Tradecraft Primer

A Framework for Aspiring Interrogators

Tradecraft Primer

Primer

A Framework
for
Aspiring
Interrogators

Paul Charles Topalian

CRC Press
Taylor & Francis Group
Boca Raton London New York

CRC Press is an imprint of the
Taylor & Francis Group, an **informa** business

U.S. Government Disclaimer: This Primer does not constitute an official release of United States government information. All statements of fact, opinion, or analysis expressed are those of the author and do not reflect the official positions or views of the U.S. Government. Nothing in the contents should be construed as asserting or implying U.S. Government authentication of information or endorsement of the author's views. This material has been reviewed solely for classification.

CRC Press
Taylor & Francis Group
6000 Broken Sound Parkway NW, Suite 300
Boca Raton, FL 33487-2742

© 2016 by Taylor & Francis Group, LLC
CRC Press is an imprint of Taylor & Francis Group, an Informa business

No claim to original U.S. Government works

Printed on acid-free paper
Version Date: 20160113

International Standard Book Number-13: 978-1-4987-5114-8 (Paperback)

Visit the Taylor & Francis Web site at
http://www.taylorandfrancis.com

and the CRC Press Web site at
http://www.crcpress.com

Contents

Preface

Whether at home or overseas, organized crime groups, enemy spies, and terrorists follow the same modus operandi. They operate in the shadows and rely on deception to evade capture and surprise to achieve their goals. Among the tools available to counter these groups is information. And often the best source of that information comes from the criminals, spies, and terrorists themselves—those captured, detained or held in lawful custody, and questioned. Yet experience tells us that such suspects and detainees do not just give up their secrets simply over tea and cookies. Sometimes, tougher measures are needed to obtain the information they possess. After all, getting the information they know allows us to take apart their networks and, quite possibly, save many thousands of lives and, most certainly, save multibillions of U.S. taxpayer dollars.

Among the arsenal of weapons at our nation's disposal to help thwart groups that endanger public safety and seek to harm our nation are our military, our law enforcement agencies, and the intelligence community—all working together as part of our country's national security team. And within these large institutions is a small subset of talented men and women who practice a secretive tradecraft few understand and even fewer have ever performed. They are called *interrogators*.

Much of what we know about the interrogation tradecraft has been passed down through the years primarily by word of mouth—in some cases over hundreds or even thousands of years—from one interrogator to the next. In more recent decades, though, the daily experiences of those engaged in law enforcement and intelligence provide valuable contributions. Meanwhile, most of the storied how-to manuals marketed by methodologists engaged in interrogation tradecraft are principally derived from a law enforcement context and often based on methodologies developed half a century or more ago.

With the attacks of 9/11 came the early rush to establish strategic interrogation centers for the many thousands of enemy combatants and terrorists captured on the battlefields of Afghanistan, Iraq, and other conflict zones, where an unfortunate pattern of harsh, coercive interrogations was initially commonplace. Among the many thousands of detainees captured over the past decade or more, an unspecified number were subjected to what a reasonable person may characterize as brutal, degrading treatment at the hands of a few military and intelligence interrogators. The public and political backlash was inevitable and palpable. Critics and human rights advocates equated the harsh treatment to torture and claimed that such practices violated the U.S. Constitution, our laws, and international obligations and treaties.

Domestic law enforcement has not been immune to the use of such tactics either. Frequent stories of police misconduct seem to originate from New York, Los Angeles, Chicago, Miami, and other major American cities, capturing headline news. Some of these recount shocking tales of psychologically—and, in some cases, physically—abusive interrogations of juveniles and adults who were subjected to unrelenting and coercive questioning.

Such realities within the interrogation profession have opened the door to a new era of research by a new crop of reformers who challenge past beliefs, the validity of previous research, and the tactics and techniques of previous generations of interrogators. This contemporary community of behavioral scientists and methodologists—both in the United States and abroad—is providing us with fresh insight into the dynamics of human motivation, deception, and truth-telling, and more effective human influence strategies and tactics. What was once thought to be valid is giving way to new findings, demonstrating that, in many cases, professed experts did not actually know what they thought they knew.

Putting the science aside, the practice of interrogation tradecraft still relies heavily on the creative talents of a single person—the interrogator—in a one-on-one highly personalized interaction with an often less than fully cooperative suspect or detainee. From that unique perspective, the tradecraft demonstrates that a successful interrogation depends on the finesse and artful skill of the interrogator, certainly assisted by behavioral science, but not entirely dependent upon it.

To succeed, the interrogator must connect on an interpersonal level and persuasively convince an uncooperative subject to disclose a valuable commodity—what the subject knows—often in opposition to the subject's own interests. To do this effectively, the interrogator must do so lawfully and ethically, in keeping with U.S. Constitutional values. No easy task.

Despite recent advances in national policy guidance, the profession continues to be the target of derision by a vocal segment of scholars, politicians, newscasters, and other pundits concerned with human rights, government transparency, and the law. Such discussions are divided over the moral, legal, and ethical arguments over many of the legacy techniques in practice, which many claim still amount to forceful coercion or worse.

Understanding what is permissible and not permissible and where to draw the line are the major reasons behind this primer. While a number of former government officials may continue to face criticism for permitting harsh treatment of those in their custody or control, the larger issue of preventing future abuse requires a sea change within the profession and in the way our interrogation programs are run and managed.

The lessons of the past several decades are clear. Effective interrogation programs require three essential elements to function properly: (1) trained, vetted, and self-disciplined interrogators; (2) unambiguous behavior or performance standards—for the *do and don'ts* inside the interrogation room; and (3) engaged managers or leaders who exercise oversight over their interrogators. In each case where violations occurred—whether in the military, law enforcement, or the intelligence community—one or more of these three elements were absent.

Whether interrogators serve in the military, in law enforcement, or in the intelligence community, they share an important goal when performing their duties. That goal is gathering useful and reliable information from an often reticent or uncooperative suspect or detainee. And based on the experiences of successful master interrogators, this is achieved most effectively by

- forging a constructive, rapport-based relationship that induces trust and cooperation between the interrogator and subject;
- preparing beforehand and asking questions in ways that help the suspect or detainee with memory recall and in ways that elicit accurate information; and
- undermining resistance and deception by effective use of approved tactics and techniques that are lawful and ethical.

Keep in mind, too, the other aims of this primer. They are to give an aspiring interrogator a leg up before entering formal training and encourage their participation in the evolving future of the profession by

- providing a baseline of where law enforcement, the military, and intelligence community stand in the art and science of interrogation tradecraft;
- identifying the most commonly authorized interrogation techniques which experts claim to yield the best chances of success;
- pointing out the many variables that influence why suspects confess or do not confess to crimes and the empirical findings associated with admissions and denials;
- advocating for a community-wide code of ethics for the profession that promotes high ethical standards for interrogators based on our nation's values, the U.S. Constitution, our laws and statutes, international agreements, and the policies of our nation's leaders; and
- inspiring interrogators to further pursue independent research and study to improve their skills.

Have a great career.

Author

 **Paul Charles Topalian** possesses nearly 30 years of experience as an intelligence professional with extensive overseas experience in Asia and Europe. His foundational expertise on the topic in this primer is built on assignments with the U.S. military, the intelligence community, and law enforcement. His academic credentials include an undergraduate degree from Norwich University and two graduate degrees—a master of science from Salve Regina University and a master of arts from the U.S. Naval War College. Find Paul at tradecraftprimer@gmail.com or at home with family and friends on the beach in Kailua, Hawaii. Aloha.

Getting Our Terms Straight

1

In its battle against transnational and domestic organized crime groups, enemy spies, and terrorists, our nation turns to its law enforcement officers, the military, and the intelligence community and conceptualizes a unified strategy against these continuously mutating and dangerous threats to our national security and our worldwide interests. One manifestation of this strategy is the cooperation that frequently takes place among them and where sharing a detainee or suspect inside the interrogation room may provide critical information to support either an ongoing law enforcement investigation or an ongoing intelligence operation, or both. As pointed out in a comprehensive Intelligence Science Board study, *Intelligence Interviewing*, (2009): "For the foreseeable future, then, the United States will need information from persons in custody who may know about matters critical to our national security."

Yet, findings to the 2008 Senate Armed Services Committee report, *Inquiry into Treatment of Detainees in U.S. Custody*, and to the 2014 follow-on partially released report from the Senate Select Committee on Intelligence, *Central Intelligence Agency's Detention and Interrogation Program*, indicate that this collaboration between law enforcement and the intelligence community had room for improvement. These Senate reports make clear that the two sides frequently disagreed over the treatment of captured terrorists and enemy alien detainees held in their custody or in their control and over interrogation practices used in overseas U.S. government detention facilities.

Over a decade of investigative reporting by U.S. and foreign news media attests to this stormy relationship, frequently pitting former officials of the Federal Bureau of Investigation (FBI) on one side of the debate and former officials of the Central Intelligence Agency (CIA) on the other side. Meanwhile, our nation's military found itself in the middle, with senior leaders of two presidential administrations—those of George W. Bush and of Barack Obama—leaning to one side or the other in these divisive discussions. To end the acrimony, the incumbent U.S. president at that moment in history, Barack Obama, personally intervened by using his executive authority.

Many saw Executive Order 13491, *Ensuring Lawful Interrogations*, which President Obama signed almost immediately after taking office in 2009, as a major step to resolve the acrimony over how our nation's interrogation programs are to be run. Others saw the executive order as a political expedient solution that only touched the surface of a very complex issue. Apparently, the intelligence community, the military, and law enforcement were operating from different frames of reference when it came to interrogation tradecraft.

The Need to Seek Common Ground

Some assert that the term *interrogation* has different technical meanings in intelligence and law enforcement, among which the military is an integral part of both, and so the two could never agree to a common standard. The assertion is false. Such a belief fails to grasp that the aims of intelligence and law enforcement interrogation methodologies are the same—to gather reliable and useful information.

For the Department of Defense, the *Army Field Manual 2–22.3* (2006), *Human Intelligence Collector Operations*, carries within it the operative definition of interrogation, now equally relied on by the entire intelligence community: "the systematic effort to procure information to answer specific collection requirements by direct and indirect questioning techniques of a person who is in the custody of the forces conducting the questioning."

Law enforcement faces a larger challenge when it comes to defining the term *interrogation*. With so many activities and agencies, including federal, state, local, tribal, and territorial entities, the closest definition that receives general acceptance among them is that found in Inbau, Reid, Buckley et al.'s *Criminal Interrogation and Confessions* which, since 1962, largely serves as the standard reference manual for investigative interviews and interrogations among the general law enforcement community. Captured from its pages, the term *interrogation* is interpreted to mean ". . . the accusatory questioning of a subject . . . involving active persuasion . . . that occurs in a controlled environment . . . when an investigator is reasonably certain of a suspect's guilt . . . for the purpose of learning the truth" (Inbau, Reid, Buckley et al. 2013).

Both definitions reflect the interests of their target audience. The 2006 *Army Field Manual*'s definition focuses on the collection of "information" principally for intelligence requirements. Meanwhile, Inbau, Reid, Buckley et al.'s definition asserts a search for the "truth" through its "accusatory" approach to questioning, a traditional approach that presumes knowledge, guilt, and deception in the subject.

Both definitions try to explain their respective approaches to interrogations in other ways, as well. The Department of Defense's definition makes reference to vague "direct and indirect" questioning techniques. Inbau, Reid,

Buckley et al.'s definition makes reference to cryptic "active persuasion" tactics. By doing so, both rely on ambiguous terms which fail to recognize the evolving nature of the interrogation tradecraft, with ever increasing demands for greater transparency and fairness and a growing public chorus who oppose the questionable interrogation practices of previous years.

Coincidentally, both definitions fail to capture an important aim of an interrogation—transforming an uncooperative or reticent subject to one who is cooperative; one that voluntarily accommodates answering the interrogator's questions with reliable and useful responses. After all, absent a recalcitrant subject, little need exists for an interrogation. Rather, for cooperative detainees and suspects basic elicitation, debriefing, or interview techniques may suffice.

In principle, then, a major step toward achieving a unified interrogation strategy and improving cooperation among law enforcement, the military, and the intelligence community, in the context of interrogations, would be to seek common ground for what is meant by the term *interrogation*.

Redefining the Term *Interrogation*

In recognition of the multiple dynamics at play, to include oversight committees and ameliorate public concerns, a suggested definition of interrogation for the profession might better read: "the *systematic* use of *authorized* techniques that influence the transition of an uncooperative subject held in *custody*, or detained in a *controlled setting*, into a cooperative source willing to respond *voluntarily* to questions that seek *reliable* and *useful* information in support of either a law enforcement investigation or intelligence requirements" (also see Meissner, Evans, Brandon et al. 2010).

The term *systematic* implies a methodical or deliberate approach tailored to the subject, the situational setting, and the information sought. The term *authorized* is interpreted to mean lawful, ethical, and permitted by current government policy. The term *custody* principally speaks to law enforcement–managed interrogations, while a *controlled setting* is common to most military- and intelligence-focused interrogations when outside of a custodial setting. The term *voluntarily* denotes the absence of coercion. The term *reliable* is interpreted to mean truthful and accurate. *Useful* is interpreted to mean relevant to an ongoing investigation or to intelligence requirements.

Keep in mind that, whether the interrogation takes place in an intelligence, military, or law enforcement context, three common features are desirable in all effective interrogations:

- First, the suspect or detainee voluntarily answers questions within his or her sphere of knowledge.
- Second, the tactics and techniques used are lawful, approved for use, and ethical.
- Third, the interrogator gains reliable information that is useful.

Comparing Law Enforcement and Intelligence Interrogations

As we just discussed, a common denominator between law enforcement and intelligence interrogations is getting reliable and useful information. For law enforcement, this typically means eliciting from a person of interest or a suspect an incriminating statement, a partial admission, or a full confession about a past criminal act of sufficient credibility and validity that it can be referred as evidence to a prosecutor. For intelligence, this often means gaining from a detainee strategic insight and knowledge or time-sensitive information—termed *actionable intelligence* (see the following figure)—about persons, places, organizations, and their associated plans; and useful to assist in future choices whether supporting our homeland defense, our deployed forces in overseas conflict zones, or our national decision-makers. In either instance, whether in a law enforcement or intelligence context, responsible interrogators also elicit statements which exonerate innocent persons held in custody; encourage leads to identify others responsible for the act or event under investigation or point to those engaged in hatching future plots; and collect additional insights which contribute to a broader understanding of the events, people, and organizations under investigation.

Actionable Intelligence
Information that is used to deter, disrupt, and defeat the ability of our enemies to endanger our nation, its citizens, our allies, and U.S. interests around the globe.

Another important factor that often distinguishes law enforcement from intelligence interrogations is the degree of public safety concern and the degree of urgency. *It's what's at stake that matters.* For instance, interrogating a probable serial killer or child molester for crimes that are clearly unconscionable pales in significance to interrogating a likely terrorist who may know of a ticking time-bomb plot that could kill many thousands of innocent citizens. As a nation of laws, however, the exigency of the circumstances and the immediate danger to society does not provide an open mandate, or the right, for an interrogator to violate the law. Under such a hypothetical scenario, the best an interrogator could hope is for the court to judge his or her liability and punishment by the totality of the facts and circumstances.

The following figure highlights many of these points.

Similarities and Differences	
Law Enforcement Interrogations	Intelligence Interrogations
• Gathering of information: essential for a criminal case—evidence and leads	• Gathering of information: essential for assessments, actionable intelligence, and leads
• Confessions: a significant achievement in the law enforcement world	• Confessions: of secondary interest to the intelligence community
• Degree of detail: sufficient to prove guilt	• Degree of detail: the more details, the better
• Responsibility: primary importance—seek sufficient information for a conviction	• Responsibility: secondary importance—knowledge is primary
• Tactics and techniques: stringent	• Tactics and techniques: flexible
• Focus: on the past	• Focus: on the future
• Degree of urgency: low to moderate	• Degree of urgency: moderate to high

Other Associative Terms

When we speak of gathering information from people, something common to both law enforcement and intelligence, a number of associative terms related to these professions are frequently used and often misunderstood. In researching them, no single source satisfactorily defined many of them. What I captured below is a synthesis of the terms.

Law Enforcement Custodial Interrogations

Within law enforcement, the terms *interrogation, custodial interview,* and *custodial interrogation* are frequently used interchangeably. Similar to an intelligence-focused interrogation, the aim is to influence the transition of an uncooperative suspect or detainee to a cooperative frame of mind, a mindset in which the subject cooperates to the questioning. And, under such a setting, the person's freedom to leave the interrogation is controlled by the government. An important point, too, law enforcement custodial interrogations require a "waiver" of *Miranda* rights to proceed, a topic further explored later in this primer. The *Miranda* warning is generally not required in intelligence interrogations of alien detainees captured on foreign battlefields.

Law Enforcement Noncustodial Interviews

A law enforcement noncustodial interview, sometimes called an investigative interview, is used to explain the systematic screening and non-accusatory questioning of persons of interest and likely suspects to obtain relevant information using basic question-and-answer or elicitation techniques. During such interviews, a law enforcement officer initially evaluates the subject for potential guilt or knowledge, relevant background information, resistance, rapport-building potential, and interpersonal and intrapersonal dynamics as a stepping stone to a tailored custodial interrogation strategy. Without a reading of the *Miranda* rights, the person in a noncustodial interview retains the right to leave at any time.

In an intelligence context, a noncustodial interview is called a pre-interrogation interview. However, unlike a law enforcement noncustodial interview, the person's right to leave a pre-interrogation interview or screening is situational dependent. As we will learn later in this primer, a far less intrusive methodology is used to interview witnesses and victims.

The following figure captures the similarities and differences between a typical law enforcement interview and a law enforcement interrogation.

Similarities and Differences	
Law Enforcement Interviews	**Law Enforcement Interrogations**
• Aims: seek reliable and useful information	• Aims: seek reliable and useful information
• Goal: simply collect information	• Goal: a confession, admission, or incriminating statement
• Process: typically nonjudgmental; elicitation	• Process: typically judgmental; accusatory
• Source: witnesses, victims, and persons of interest	• Source: suspects of crimes
• Initial expectation: truthfulness presumed	• Initial expectation: deceit presumed
• Structure: reasonable start and end times	• Structure: no set time limits
• Tone: casual; polite; even tempered; empathetic	• Tone: formal; persuasive; confident; assertive
• Freedom to depart: retained by subject	• Freedom to depart: retained by government
• Setting: noncustodial; voluntary	• Setting: custodial; controlled
• Version of events: respondent's side of the story	• Version of events: investigator's hypothesis
• *Miranda* warning: waiver not required	• *Miranda* warning: waiver required

Elicitation

An *elicitation* is a subtle and sophisticated question-and-answer technique commonly used to uncover additional information that is not otherwise known and shielded by the respondent. The communication exchange can be face-to-face during a casual conversation, but may also be over the phone, or in writing (e.g., text, tweet, or e-mail). Often integrated into the interrogation process once an uncooperative suspect transitions to a cooperative mindset, it calls for a softer, less confrontational demeanor and measured tone of voice. Moreover, it serves as a dominant question-and-answer technique during the interview process when working with victims and witnesses. In most cases, the respondent is witting to the purpose of the questioning. In other instances, the respondent may be unwitting to the underlying and indirect fact-finding aims of the question.

Strategic Debriefings

Debriefing is a term that is frequently heard in intelligence circles and is interpreted to mean the systematic questioning of a responsive and cooperative individual by intelligence officers whether outside or inside a custodial or controlled setting. Its aim is to elicit information volunteered in a direct, nonconfrontational, and business-like manner in response to intelligence collection requirements. In some cases, incentives or inducements may be used to achieve and reward cooperation. In other cases, disincentives may be used. Similarly as in elicitation, the respondent may be witting to the aims of the underlying questions or, in other instances, may be unwitting to the true aims of the person asking the question.

Tactical Questioning

Tactical questioning is the field-expedient initial questioning of a captured or detained person at or near the point of capture by the military for information of immediate tactical value and before the individual is placed in a detention facility. According to the Department of Defense doctrine, tactical questioning is limited to direct questioning and is an unstated exception to the rule that only officially trained personnel may perform interrogations and debriefings.

Confessions

A *confession* is a self-incriminating statement by a suspect admitting or acknowledging guilt and direct participation in a crime. Among police officers, it is often loosely interpreted to mean any statements which tie a suspect to a crime.

Admissions

An *admission* is far less specific than a criminal confession. It might include acknowledgment by a suspect to some facts implying some degree of guilt or involvement in the crime under investigation but falls short of a full confession.

For more explanations of other associated legal terms, I suggest you explore *Black's Law Dictionary*, which serves as the most comprehensive and authoritative source of such terminology. For the most relevant military and intelligence terms, the *Department of Defense Dictionary of Military and Associated Terms* (Joint Publication 1-02) and its companion glossary *Joint Intelligence* (Joint Publication 2-0) are available online at http://www.dtic.mil/doctrine.

Interrogation's Tortuous Past

2

Interrogation and torture have been linked since antiquity and, in a historical context, commonly practiced by those exercising absolute power over those they ruled or held in captivity. Despite the passage of thousands of years, the two remain synonymous in the eyes of many people, even though torture and interrogations are distinctly dissimilar.

Torture, along with other forms of cruel, inhumane, and abusive treatment or punishment, is illegal by the U.S. Constitution, our laws, and recognized as an international human rights crime. On the other hand, the practice of interrogation tradecraft remains a legitimate and essential law enforcement, military, and intelligence skill.

Where interrogation and torture are still practiced together by lawless state and nonstate actors, the threads that commonly link them are severe physical or mental pain or suffering for the victim. This disturbing legacy demonstrates that torture serves as an expedient tool of interrogators for the following major reasons:

- Breaking free will, such as getting the person to say or do something he or she would otherwise not say or do; make a confession, admit guilt, or agree to support a propaganda campaign.
- Punishing and intimidating others and, in the process, exerting authority, exacting revenge, deterring revolt, or serving as a warning.
- Enforcing submission or conversion to a new religion or ideology.

Today, we know through a number of landmark studies that exerting mental or physical coercion during an interrogation produces unreliable results. As pointed out in the 2008 Senate Armed Services Committee report on the treatment of detainees by the U.S. military, put a person under enough discomfort or pain and he or she will eventually say whatever it takes to stop it. And, sure, harsh treatment may increase the amount of information the person will tell the interrogator but it does not mean that the information is accurate. In fact, harsh treatment usually decreases the reliability of the information. Of course, there are exceptions, like with all generalizations, but they are not common. Rather, the likelihood that harsh mistreatment during an interrogation will increase accurate information from a detainee or suspect is very low. And, as we will learn later in this primer, there is also the likelihood that the use of excessive physical pain and extreme mental suffering may further harden defensive resistance in uncooperative subjects (U.S. Congress 2008).

Snapshots from Distant History

The Qin Dynasty

The first documented government to rely on torture as a political tool was the Qin (pronounced "chin") Dynasty, the empire which unified China under a single emperor. A time of extreme cruelty and violence, the dynasty came to power under the leadership of Emperor Qin Shi Huang Di (260–210 BCE).

To forge his nation, the emperor ruled under a tyrannical form of government called *legalism*—a practice in which everyone was terrified and informants were everywhere. Death, maiming, and torture were used as punishments for the slightest infractions—foreshadowing the Cultural Revolution two millennia later. Along with his political critics and military opponents, the emperor singled out intellectuals, in particular, for special persecution along with their books, especially the followers of Confucius.

The Roman Empire

Two hundred years later, the West experienced its own form of tyranny under the Roman Empire, most vividly represented by the reign of Caligula (AD 37–41), who relied on torture to punish anyone he mistrusted. Other cruel rulers soon followed in near succession, such as Nero (AD 54–68) and Commodus (AD 180–192), whose reigns likewise relied on torture and persecutions against those they considered enemies of the Roman state—especially Christians, political opponents, and criminals alike.

Crucifixions, stoning, floggings, and death in the arena were the most publicly recognized form of punishment and torture. Yet an infinite variety of other forms were also practiced under Roman rulers, limited only by their imagination. We know some of them today by such strange-sounding Latin-based names as *flagellation*, *decimation*, and *precipitation*.

Still, other forms of torture were adopted from their Greek predecessors, such as the Sicilian bull. Here, victims were placed inside a closed chamber made of bronze and basically baked to death over a fire. Their screams accentuated by specially designed honed baffles.

The Dark Ages

The collapse of the Roman Empire coincided with the rise of the Dark Ages, roughly from the 6th to the 13th century. It was a period in medieval Europe in which the art of interrogation and torture reached a heightened level of sophistication under the union of the church and the state. Under the Grand Inquisition, heretics were nearly always subjected to coercive physical and psychological abuse, and, in many cases, pain by the Catholic Church, and, if found guilty, were then turned over to the state for final punishment (Educing Information 2006).

The first how-to interrogation manuals appeared at this time. Prominent among them was *Practica inquisitionis heretice pravitatis*, translated as "Conduct of the inquisition into heretical depravity." Written in 1323 by Dominican priest Bernard Gui, inquisitor of Toulouse in southern France, his manual covers the nature and types of heresy an inquisitor might encounter and it provides advice on everything from conducting an interrogation to pronouncing a death sentence. A prodigious writer, the portfolio demonstrates that Gui was methodical, learned, clever, patient, and persistent—the ideal qualities for an interrogator even today.

A generation after Gui, another Dominican priest, Nicholas Eymerich, produced the *Directorium Inquisitorum*, which became the definitive handbook of the Spanish Inquisition. Eymerich served as inquisitor general of Aragon in the 1350s. Built on the work of his French predecessor, Eymerich's detailed treatise achieved even greater popularity and served inquisitors well into the 17th century.

Eymerich makes a point to warn inquisitors to expect deception from those being questioned and lays out the ways heretics will employ resistance. They include equivocation, redirecting the question, feigning astonishment, twisting the meaning of words, changing the subject, feigning illness, and feigning stupidity. To counter such ruses, Eymerich writes, the well-prepared inquisitor has tricks of his or her own. For example, to confront a resistant or deceptive prisoner, the inquisitor might sit with a large stack of bogus documents in front of him or her, which he or she would pretend to consult as he or she asks questions or listens to answers, periodically looking up from the pages as if they contradicted the testimony and saying, "It is clear to me that you are hiding the truth." This same technique survives today in a number of training manuals. Another technique suggested by Eymerich is for the inquisitor to suddenly shift tactics away from a harsh demeanor and feign empathy and understanding, perhaps even offering food or a drink. Today, we call this the *good cop/bad cop technique*.

Other such techniques included threatening heretics with death or injury, playing on the prisoner's feelings of utter despair and futility, and reminding the detainee that only cooperation with the interrogator offers the heretic a path to something better. Not surprisingly, inquisitors also believed that extended solitary confinement was one of the most influential interrogation techniques for breaking a person. We saw many of these same techniques—noncoercive and coercive—reappearing nearly 600 years later in the war against terrorism, some labeled "enhanced interrogation techniques."

Salem Witch Trials

Not unique to the Inquisition, some of the same practices were later adopted by the Puritans during the Salem witch trials, which, once again, reaffirmed the unity of religious and secular authorities for the colony. We also see, in a number of cases, the use of fire and water to purify the defendants and uncover the "truth." Accused citizens of Salem were offered two options: they could plead guilty or innocent. The majority of the people under questioning admitted guilt and usually ended with the least punitive forms of colonial punishment: the wearing of letters such as *T* for thief, *A* for adulterers, and *D* for drunkards; whippings; or time in the stocks and pillory. However, should a defendant assert innocence, that was when things really got serious.

Some of the more common methods of interrogation and torture included the dunking stool. With a setup similar to a seesaw, the accused was on one end which would hang above the local pond, while on the other end stood the accusers. They would repeatedly dunk their victim under the water. If the victims floated, they were a witch under the assumption that they used magic to stay afloat. Ironically, if they sank and nearly drowned, they were innocent.

Although the legend of Salem witch trials claims victims burning at the stake, in reality, most met their fate by hanging on Gallows Hill. Between 1692 and 1693, more than two hundred people were accused of practicing the "devil's magic," or witchcraft, and 19 were executed by hanging; one was crushed to death.

Napoleon Speaks Out!

More than a century after the Puritans, one of history's most famous military leaders stands tall for condemning the practice of torture. By this time, torture is clearly used on the battlefield to exact intelligence. In a blunt letter, Napoleon Bonaparte chastised Major General Louis-Alexandre Berthier for mistreating his prisoners during the 1798 French military campaign in Egypt:

[The] barbarous custom of whipping men suspected of having important secrets to reveal must be abolished. It has always been recognized that this method of interrogation, by putting men to the torture, is useless. The wretches say whatever comes into their heads and whatever they think one wants to believe. Consequently, the Commander-in-Chief forbids the use of a method which is contrary to reason and humanity. (Plon 1861)

The Wickersham Commission

Throughout the 19th and the early 20th century, coercive interrogation practices, called the *third degree*, were common in police stations throughout America. Beginning in the early 1920s, however, the public's concern over lawless police practices in the country steadily grew to the point where President Hoover appointed former Attorney General George Wickersham to chair the 1929 National Commission on Law Observance and Law Enforcement.

In 1931, this body, commonly known as the Wickersham Commission, issued the *Report on Lawlessness in Law Enforcement*, among its 14-volume report on criminal justice in America. The report became a catalyst for modern police reform. Documenting various abuses, the Wickersham Commission concluded that the police use of brutal physical force, threats, intimidation, and protracted incommunicado detention during interrogations was widespread. In short, the *third degree* was a common practice in most of America's police departments.

What is the *third degree*? This term is a euphemism for a variety of harsh, even brutal, interrogation tactics used by police to extract information from a suspect. It relied on physical force to inflict injury and pain and on psychological threats to cause duress to extract confessions from vulnerable suspects. The significance of the *third degree* was more than just a representation of abusive police practices that violated constitutionally protected civil liberties of persons taken under police custody. Equally as well, it represented an off-the-record system of dispensing extrajudicial punishment by the police on victims (Leo 1992).

The Wickersham reports made their intended impact. Physically coercive interrogation methods gradually began to decline in use by police departments starting in the mid-1930s. In place of the *third degree*, the police began to adopt methodologies that relied on ever subtle and increasingly sophisticated manipulation, persuasion, and deception techniques to induce confessions and admissions from subjects in custodial interrogations (Leo 1992). By the mid-1970s, such tactics became the standard police practice across the country. Although we still hear about police abuses during custodial questioning, the reported use of the *third degree* during interrogations is far less frequent than in the past. Its use today is considered an aberration.

Such an anomaly popped up in 2010 during the trial of a senior Chicago police officer, Lieutenant Jon Burge, who commanded the Violent Crime Unit of Chicago's Area Two Headquarters. For decades, city prosecutors dismissed complaints about his command where suspects were being coerced into making false confessions—at gunpoint, with shocks to the genitals, or with plastic bags over their heads. In 2011, Officer Burge was sentenced to jail for deceptively lying about his penchant for the cruel use of torture on suspects. Dozens of cases are now under review along with $5.5 million in reparations expected for his victims (Chicago Tribune, Online Editions: Jan 22, 2011 and Apr 14, 2015, Search: Jon Burge).

Evolving Case Law

Court-driven legal rulings continue to play an important role in influencing police interrogation practices. In the past century, in particular, a number of watershed rulings elaborated and enforced constitutional rights and due process norms and sought to restrain police abuse. The use of force, threats of harm, denial of food or sleep, prolonged isolation, and badgering by multiple interrogators over extended hours or even days are no longer condoned by legal authorities. By excluding confessions that are the by-product of physically or psychologically coercive methods, the courts sought to stamp out third degree interrogation practices in America.

Brown versus Mississippi (1936)
and Chambers versus Florida (1940)

Despite the Fifth, Eighth, and Fourteenth Amendments of the Constitution, state courts were slow to recognize that coercive interrogation-induced confessions were inadmissible. In *Brown versus Mississippi* (1936), the Supreme Court held, in the first series of state cases, that physically coerced confessions were not admissible but had to be voluntary to be admitted into evidence. In other words, the due process clause of the 14th Amendment prevents the prosecution from using information in a confession that resulted from the use of physical force by law enforcement officers. A follow-on ruling in 1940 by the Supreme Court in *Chambers versus Florida* (1940) held that some forms of psychological pressure could be interpreted as equally coercive. In this case, the suspect was first threatened by mob violence and then grilled by four interrogators over five consecutive days until he relented and confessed. Since then, police practices, such as threats of harm or punishment, excessively lengthy interrogations, promises of leniency, and denial of sleep and food, are considered presumptively coercive.

Rochin versus California (1952)

In *Rochin versus California* (1952), the U.S. Supreme Court established the "shock-the-conscience" test. Through its interpretation of the Fourteenth Amendment, the Court ruling in *Rochin* prohibits depriving any person of "life, liberty, or property without the due process of law" and prohibits shocking actions by agents of the government that fall outside the standards of civilized decency.

In *Rochin*, three California law enforcement officers busted into the room of Antonio Rochin under suspicion that he was selling narcotics. Fearing arrest, Rochin quickly swallowed two morphine capsules on a nightstand next to his bed. Wrestled to the ground, Rochin was next taken to a hospital where he was forcedly induced to vomit the pills. Charged and convicted of narcotics charges, Rochin tried to get the evidence of the capsules suppressed.

On an appeal, Supreme Court Justice Felix Frankfurter held that the conduct by the California law enforcement officers "shocks the conscience" and the "canons of decency and fairness." Their actions offended even those with "hardened sensibilities." They were representative of "methods too close to the rack and screw." The Court also emphasized that the same prohibition extends to federal government officials under the due process provisions of the Fifth Amendment.

Miranda versus Arizona (1966)

Nearly 30 years after *Chambers*, the Supreme Court's landmark ruling in *Miranda versus Arizona* (1966) held that the police have a responsibility to protect a suspect's Fifth and Sixth Amendment rights during a custodial interrogation. The Court's decision in *Miranda* addressed four different cases involving custodial interrogations. In each of these cases, the unrepresented defendant was questioned by police officers, detectives, or a prosecuting attorney in a room in which he was cut off from the outside world. In none of these cases was the defendant given a full and effective warning of his rights at the outset of the interrogation process. In all the cases, the questioning elicited admissions and, in three of them, signed statements were admitted at trial.

The *Miranda* ruling served as a stepping-stone to a new era in law enforcement doctrine. In taking the *Miranda* case, the Supreme Court determined the future role that the police have in protecting the rights of the accused guaranteed by the Fifth Amendment right against self-incrimination and the Sixth Amendment right to an attorney. The Supreme Court ruled 5–4 in favor of Miranda. This pivotal decision gave rise to what has become known as the *Miranda* rights warning.

While many jurisdictions have their own regulations as to the precise rights warning given to a person interrogated in police custody, the typical rights warning has four basic elements reflected in the following figure, and should conclude with the statement "Do you understand these rights as they have been read to you?"

Standard *Miranda* Rights Warning
1. You have the right to remain silent.
2. Anything you say can and will be used against you in a court of law.
3. You have the right to an attorney.
4. If you cannot afford an attorney, one will be appointed for you.
Based on *Miranda versus Arizona*, 384 U.S. 436, 1966.

As part of the *Miranda* ruling, Chief Justice Earl Warren condemned what he saw as the trend toward increasingly manipulative, deceptive, and psychologically coercive tactics relied on by the police to elicit confessions from defendants during custodial interrogations. The following figure captures some of the major concerns expressed by Chief Justice Warren as part of the *Miranda* ruling.

Criticized Deceptive Police Tactics
• Persistent, lengthy, and aggressively hostile questioning
• Undermining the relevance of the Fifth and Sixth Amendment rights
• Offering the subject legal and moral excuses for the act by casting blame on others or society
• Manipulating the subject's psychological vulnerabilities
• Implying promises that cannot be met
• Fabricating false evidence by false witnesses
• Using empathy to misrepresent a police officer's true intentions
Modified from *Miranda versus Arizona*, 384 U.S. 436, 1966.

To offset these manipulative tactics, the *Miranda* ruling also requires the police seek a "waiver" from the subject before a custodial interrogation can legally begin. Additionally, such waivers must be granted "voluntarily" and "knowingly." The two requirements are exacerbated when the English language is not the suspect's primary spoken language, there is no interpreter on the scene, and when cultural dynamics come into play. Unless such a waiver is obtained and understood by the subject, an interrogation is presumed coercive and the statements made during the interrogation are inadmissible.

As to the waiver, all the police officer needs to do after reading the *Miranda* warning is state, "I would like to talk to you about matter XYZ. Is this OK?" If the subject expresses a willingness to talk, the interrogation may proceed. If, however, the subject refuses to talk or asks for an attorney, the interrogation must terminate. Moreover, it is not permissible to pressure subjects into waiving their *Miranda* rights. And, if after beginning the interrogation a subject decides to change his or her mind and invokes *Miranda*, the interrogation must terminate immediately.

Despite Chief Justice Warren's concerns, once a suspect waives his or her rights, a multitude of tactics open up to law enforcement, many of which may appear unethical but legal. For instance, police interrogators may tell the suspect that the murder victim is still alive; exaggerate or downplay the seriousness of the offense; tell the suspect that they have convincing evidence of his or her guilt; tell the suspect that they are investigating one crime when, in fact, they are investigating another; tell the suspect that a polygraph test indicates guilt when it does not; or fake compassion, empathy, and friendship to elicit confessions from the suspect.

Of course, there are limits to police deception. For instance, a police interrogator or investigator cannot trick a criminal suspect into waiving his or her *Miranda* rights; fabricate tangible false evidence, such as a forensics report claiming the suspect's fingerprints were on a weapon; or lie in the courtroom in front of a judge. Beyond this, police deception and persuasive ploys aimed at getting a confession are governed by the due process clause of the Fourteenth Amendment and only when it violates fundamental concepts of "fairness or egregious police misconduct" (Skolnick & Leo 1992).

Lessons from World War II

The Second World War elevated the importance of the interrogation tradecraft. In support of both theaters of war—the Pacific and Europe—and even stateside, the U.S. military established a number of strategic interrogation centers where high-value enemy prisoners of war (POWs) underwent systematic questioning by skilled interrogators.

In the Pacific, we found ourselves at war against the Japanese—a people, a culture, and a psychology profoundly different from our own. Fewer yet understood their language. From a military perspective, the Japanese were seen as fanatics, true believers ready to die for their emperor and in their total commitment to the bushido code—one that emphasized a no-surrender warrior mind-set epitomized by the myth of the samurai.

In the face of these challenges, the U.S. military implemented a successful interrogation strategy—one for the army and another for the navy—which was initially built on the limited cultural and linguistic skills available. The U.S. Army largely capitalized on the native language skills of *nisei*—second-generation American citizens of Japanese descent fluent in their parents' native language and born here. They largely served as enlisted members. Meanwhile, the U.S. Navy initially relied on a cadre of formally trained officers; those who previously trained as attachés and former American missionaries who served previously in Japan.

Meanwhile, as German troops entered Paris in 1940, plans were drawn up to surge interrogators against Germany. Formal training of interrogators destined for Europe began in 1942 at Fort Ritchie, Maryland. Basically a "Dale Carnegie" approach to interrogation, the course emphasized that a cigarette or a cup of coffee would frequently elicit more accurate and usable information than threats. Like the United States' effort to capitalize on *nisei* in the Pacific, the strategic interrogation plans against Germany called for recruiting recent immigrants from Europe in the United States or their children who were fluent in their parents' native language. Significant numbers were Jews who fled Germany in the past several decades or less. Nicknamed the *Ritchie Boys*, after their training center, most of them welcomed the opportunity to return to Europe in the war against Hitler and the Nazi army.

While many interrogators on all sides of the war most certainly relied on brutal and coercive tactics to get the information sought, anecdotal evidence demonstrates that the most consistently successful among them, such as U.S. Marine Major Sherwood Moran in the Pacific and even the respected German Luftwaffe and Nazi master interrogator Hanns Scharff (Interrogation: World War II, Vietnam, and Iraq 2008), recognized the inherent value of the following:

- Treating the enemy prisoners as human beings.
- Offering empathy and understanding.
- Ensuring their prisoners had access to food, clothing, and medical care.
- Relying on the power of psychology as a tool in interrogations.
- Avoiding humiliation, excessive coercion, and torture.

Unfortunately, the historical legacy and valuable lessons learned from our nation's successful military interrogation strategy of World War II were lost on a new generation of American recruits who were largely unprepared for our upcoming battles against Communism, the Iron Curtain, and the Cold War. By 1950, for example, the army had fallen from over eight million men and women at its height in the war to less than 600,000 soldiers. In the near frantic demobilization of our military after the war, most of our experienced interrogators returned home to assimilate back to civilian life. This loss in talent had profound implications on training future generations of interrogators for many decades ahead.

The Cold War Era

The U.S. Experience in the Korean War

The Communist show trials of captured U.S. aviators during the Korean War opened a national debate: How could U.S. service members confess to dropping bombs filled with germs on civilian populations when these events did not occur? Were they *brainwashed*—a term first popularized by psychologist Edward Hunter in 1951—or were they traitors? Researchers Hinkle and Wolff (1957) concluded that there was no evidence that drugs, hypnosis, or special devices had any significance in the interrogations—such as that depicted in the movie *The Manchurian Candidate*. The overwhelming conclusion of their studies was that the Soviets and the Chinese were using traditional police interrogation tactics.

About the same time Hinkle and Wolff released their research, Farber, Harlow, and West (1957) released a book that described what American POWs experienced during their confinement at the hands of the North Koreans and Chinese. Farber, Harlow, and West creatively coined the phrase "debility, dependency, and dread" to explain what American military prisoners experienced at the hands of their captors. *Debility* was induced by conditions such as semistarvation, fatigue, and disease. Control of their basic needs created *dependency*. *Dread* was marked by intense fear and anxiety.

Today, psychologists and doctors engaged in treating those in recovery from traumatic life events, typical of extreme coercive physical and psychological interrogation tactics when experienced over a prolonged period, rely on other terms—captured in the following figure—to describe their impact on at-risk or vulnerable persons.

Consequences of Physical and Psychological Trauma

- Posttraumatic stress disorder manifested by prolonged, recurring flashbacks and nightmares; significant impairment and instability in life functions; suicidal tendencies; and weakened physical health

- Depressive disorders manifested in self-destructive and suicidal thoughts and behavior

- Psychosis, in the form of delusions, bizarre ideations and behaviors, perceptual distortions, and paranoia

Adapted from *Leave No Marks: Enhanced Interrogation Techniques and the Risk of Criminality*, Physicians for Human Rights and Human Rights First, Washington, DC, 2007.

However, not everyone exposed to brutal interrogations or mistreatment will experience the anxiety of posttraumatic stress disorder or descend into psychosis or related mental illnesses. People vary and so do their psychological risk factors or vulnerabilities and their tolerance to stress, pain or terror, and to extreme fear brought about by threats of death, mutilation, or rape.

On the Heels of the Vietnam Conflict

In response to the experiences of captured aviators in the Korean War, the U.S. government started research on defensive techniques under an early 1960s Air Force contract to help with survival, evasion, resistance, and escape (SERE) training for downed pilots.

Almost simultaneously, while the Air Force-sponsored research into defensive techniques, the CIA took an alternate path. The Agency began exploring offensive interrogation techniques. Among the research, it probed the use of chemicals and drugs, sensory deprivation, hypnosis, and a multitude of other unconventional methods to enhance interrogation outcomes. This secretive program, codenamed MKULTRA, failed to achieve mainstream acceptance and, upon its discovery, the U.S. Congress shut it down.

Some of MKULTRA's major findings were captured in the infamous *KUBARK Counterintelligence Interrogation Manual* (1963), whose publication happened to coincide near the start of the Vietnam conflict. Declassified in 1997, the *KUBARK Manual* served as the intelligence community's interrogation primer for its time.

Despite the continuing criticism heaped on it, the *KUBARK Manual* contains some valuable guidance among its pages for today's interrogators:

- Develop rapport with the detainee.
- Treat each detainee as a unique individual.
- Tailor interrogations to a detainee's personality.

Importantly, too, the *KUBARK Manual* encouraged interrogators to ask themselves, "How can I make the subject want to tell me what he or she knows?" rather than, "How can I trap him or her into disclosing what he or she knows?" And it also offers this advice to interrogators: "[T]he KUBARK questioner should aim not for a personal triumph but for his true goal—the acquisition of all needed information by any authorized means."

Ultimately, the *KUBARK Manual* lost standing within the intelligence community and the military. Operating on limited research in offensive interrogation strategies, the writers adopted harsh SERE training tactics to meet many of its operational requirements. In doing so, the authors failed to fully appreciate the artificiality of SERE-derived training scenarios, which sought to train our aviators in resistance techniques in opposition to coercive Communist Chinese, North Korean, and Soviet interrogation tactics—tactics that clearly conflicted with American values, our Constitution, and the Geneva Conventions. Importantly, too, the *KUBARK Manual's* characterization of human personality types lacked a sound basis in empirical-based psychology.

Reflecting on why SERE training techniques make poor role models for interrogations, the Senate Armed Forces Committee in its *Inquiry into the Treatment of Detainees Held in U.S. Custody* (2008), echoed nearly the same shortcomings identified as a weakness in the *KUBARK Manual* decades earlier:

- First, SERE lesson plans and techniques routinely employ a wide range of coercive methods that often fall well outside of U.S. laws, the Geneva Conventions, and other international treaties and human rights guidelines.
- Second, although questioning is an important element of role play exercises, this activity during SERE training does not reach the depth required for either law enforcement investigations or for intelligence-focused operations.
- Third, SERE instructors, although talented, lack the expertise expected of fully trained interrogators or investigators.

Most importantly, though, the Communist interrogation techniques, which served as a model for SERE training and adopted by the intelligence community, were never intended to elicit reliable and useful information from American prisoners. Rather, their goal was to beat down American POWs to the point where they reluctantly participated in Communist propaganda campaigns against our nation.

The U.S. Experience in the Vietnam Conflict

Like our recent experiences in Iraq and Afghanistan, the Vietnam conflict was characterized by a widespread insurgency and asymmetrical warfare. A defining characteristic of an insurgency is the ability of insurgents to transition quickly between the roles of combatant and civilian, making it extremely difficult to identify the innocent from the enemy (Interrogation: World War II, Vietnam, and Iraq 2008).

Unable to easily identify discrete targets—dressed largely like the general population—U.S. military forces were limited in their ability to successfully capitalize on their massive firepower. As in Iraq and Afghanistan, interrogators were urgently needed to assist in identifying insurgents as well as their bases, plans, targets, tactics, and supply routes.

Historians typically identify the Vietnam conflict in terms of a failed counterinsurgency strategy. So, too, was the overall interrogation strategy that supported forces in the field. Among its failures, the interrogation strategy

- Alienated the local Vietnamese population through its harsh methods on innocent civilians and legitimate captives alike; and
- Lacked sufficient preparatory training for the interrogators. Many were unfamiliar with the culture, laws, customs, and language of Vietnam.

While there were certainly exceptions among the interrogators and their methodologies—for one, Army Warrant Officer Sedgwick Tourison, who authored *Talking with Victor Charlie: An Interrogator's Story* (1991)—the Cold War interrogation techniques in Korea and Vietnam largely failed to offer future generations of interrogators a valuable legacy. As a consequence, America was little prepared for what was about to emerge in the upcoming conflicts in the Middle East.

Enter the Global War on Terror

The Gulf War (1990 to 1991) and the Bosnian conflict (1992 to 1995) saw little advancements in the interrogation tradecraft. Direct military engagements in these conflicts proved too short to sustain a surge in interrogator recruitment, training, and operations.

The 2001 attacks of September 11, or 9/11, and their aftermath were a different matter. The horror of watching television footage of innocent men and women jumping out of New York City's World Trade Towers and their collapse, followed by news footage of the Pentagon attack, and then learning of United Flight 93's crash in a remote cornfield in Shanksville, Pennsylvania, made a lasting imprint on America's psyche. Together, the three events represented the largest ever foreign attack against the U.S. homeland. The fear of further attacks was pervasive, as was the need to seek answers to urgent questions. Who attacked us? Why? What did they want? What else were they planning?

The response was clear. We were at war with an enemy unlike any other. With the encouragement of the American public and the U.S. Congress—and bolstered by the Joint Resolution of September 18, 2001, which authorized the use of "all necessary force"—our nation's leaders used their mandate to unleash every available tool in our national security arsenal to gather intelligence and respond militarily to the terrorists—to do whatever it took to prevent the next attack. The gloves came off and the Department of Defense and the CIA responded. Just a day prior to the Congressional Joint Resolution, on September 17, 2001, President George W. Bush had signed a covert action

Memorandum of Notification. Under its authority, the CIA started putting in place plans to capture, detain, and interrogate high-value terrorist members of al-Qaeda who may possess critical, actionable intelligence needed to stop further attacks against our homeland, our allies, and our interests worldwide (U.S. Congress 2014).

Military internment facilities in Afghanistan, Cuba, Iraq, and elsewhere soon exploded with battlefield detainees awaiting interrogation. Operating with limited resources, many of these facilities were largely staffed by military members, law enforcement officers, contractors, psychologists, SERE advisors, linguists, analysts, and intelligence personnel inexperienced with managing large-scale, long-term prisoner holding facilities. Many lacked substantive interrogation skill sets, target familiarity, cultural awareness, and necessary linguistic skills. All were working under intense pressure to uncover actionable intelligence useful to protect our nation from further attacks and helpful to field commanders in the conflict zones—Afghanistan and Iraq.

Both programs—within the military and within the CIA—were supported by a February 7, 2002, presidential memo entitled *Humane Treatment of al-Qaeda and Taliban Detainees*, which denied al-Qaeda detainees formal protections of the Geneva Conventions and Common Article 3 based on their non-state actor status. On the other hand, the Taliban, while offered some of the protections of the Geneva Conventions because of their former association with the government of Afghanistan, were denied traditional enemy POW status because, like al-Qaeda, they wore no uniforms, attacked civilians and military alike, and failed to comply with traditional laws of war.

Renditions

Extradition is a process in which persons suspected of criminal activity are involuntarily transferred from one country to another—to those which possessed legitimate arrest warrants for their detention and trial. It is typically preceded by a formal legal process established by a bilateral treaty between countries. Other related but dissimilar terms include *deportation*, in which aliens residing in the United States are removed after an administrative hearing for violations of immigration laws; and *repatriation* or *resettlement*, in which persons voluntarily agree to relocate to their nation of origin or to a host country willing to offer asylum. Far less common, though, is the U.S. government's involuntary transfer of individuals through a process known as *rendition*. Unlike traditional extradition, persons subjected to rendition typically have no access to the judicial system of the sending country through which they may challenge their transfers. And, during President George W. Bush's administration, involuntary renditions took a prominent place within our nation's counterterrorism strategy. Human rights advocates and critics of the administration claimed that the transfers were often to countries that permitted harsh interrogation techniques prohibited in the United States, including torture. In response, the administration did not deny that renditions took place—a practice that had been in effect since 1986—but denied allegations that renditions were for purposes of torture (Garcia 2009).

Black Sites

Complementing the rendition program were efforts to remove prominent al-Qaeda and Taliban operational planners and associates—about 119 high-value terrorists in total—from their spheres of influence or power, whether on or off the battlefield, and ship them to remote, covert holding facilities, nicknamed *black sites*, where they were held incommunicado by the CIA for follow-up questioning. In other instances, some were held in Department of Defense–managed detention facilities; and, in other cases, some were transferred to liaison partners willing to accept them for questioning (U.S. Congress 2014).

Enhanced Interrogation Techniques

Among those held at black sites, a handful of hardened, uncooperative terrorist detainees assessed with knowledge of time-sensitive and actionable intelligence or knowledge of Usama bin Laden's location were subjected to *enhanced interrogation techniques* (see the following figure)—a program managed by the CIA with the approval of the president, the National Security Council, and the U.S. Department of Justice, and with the knowledge of key members of the U.S. Congress. The underlying aim of the program was to serve as a softening-up tool for the most recalcitrant among the captured senior terrorist leaders in an effort to overcome their resistance and transition them from an uncooperative to a cooperative frame of mind in preparation for debriefings and follow-up questioning (U.S. Congress 2014).

Examples of Former CIA "Standard" and "Enhanced" Interrogation Techniques	
• Attention grasp	• Sleep deprivation
• Facial hold and slap	• Waterboarding
• Sensory deprivation–darkness	• Use of diapers and nudity
• Cramped confinement	• Extended isolation
• Stress positions	• Sensory bombardment–light and sound

Extracted from *Guidelines on Medical and Psychological Support to Rendition, Interrogation, and Detention*, CIA Office of Medical Services, 2004, released and declassified in 2005.

Initially lacking in basic interrogation competencies and adequately equipped internment facilities, detainee abuses and mistreatment among some of those held were a predictable outcome—even several deaths. Moreover, at least as controversial as some of the interrogation tactics or techniques, detainees held incommunicado in undisclosed black sites were outside of the visible protection of the International Committee of the Red Cross—a recognized responsibility given it by international treaties such as the Geneva Conventions.

Predictably, the Bush administration soon found itself under challenge. In the 2006 case of *Hamdan versus Rumsfeld*, the U.S. Supreme Court rejected the Bush administration's February 2002 position that the Geneva Conventions and Common Article 3 were not applicable to the present armed conflict with al-Qaeda. The *Hamdan* ruling also denied the right of the president to convene military commissions or tribunals to prosecute select terrorists imprisoned at Guantanamo without U.S. Congressional legislation.

As a result of the *Hamdan* case, policy debates also surfaced among some Congressional lawmakers over criminal liabilities that CIA officers could possibly face for the harsh interrogation tactics approved for their use at that time. To mitigate such challenges, George W. Bush officially asserted his presidential authority in July 2007 and signed Executive Order 13440, *Interpretation of the Geneva Conventions Common Article 3 as Applied to a Program of Detention and Interrogation Operated by the Central Intelligence Agency*.

The executive order formally declared al-Qaeda and Taliban unlawful enemy and non-state actors, and, therefore, not entitled to protections as state-sponsored prisoners of war under the Third Geneva Convention. On the other hand, the President acceded to apply Common Article 3 standards to detention and interrogation programs managed by the CIA in keeping with the Supreme Court's *Hamdan* ruling.

Critics of the Bush administration often fail to recall the national security context in which the CIA operated its rendition, detention, and interrogation program on behalf of our nation. For the most part, these high-value detainees served as second or third tier terrorist operatives and facilitators within al-Qaeda and the Taliban, whose organizations posed a serious threat of violence or death to our citizens, our military, and, in the case of al-Qaeda, our nation. In other cases, some detainees served as principal planners for secondary attacks or knew of others who were doing the planning, while others knew of supporting logistical and financial networks. The security of our nation depended on our ability to learn what these people knew (CIA 2014).

In the frantic rush to stop these terrorists and go after timely intelligence, legal advisors in the Department of Justice and the White House blurred and stretched interpretations of fundamental rights given to all persons—terrorists included—embedded in our nation's Constitution, our laws, and international treaties. We needed to put away the gloves—at least partially—and we did.

Recognizing the need to modify its operations, CIA had already set in motion a number of internal reforms for its rendition, interrogation, and detainee program. Waterboarding stopped in 2003. And the last detainee to experience an enhanced interrogation was in 2007. Meanwhile, largely as a consequence of international pressure, a number of black sites had begun to close. Some detainees were released; others were transferred to countries willing to accept them or to countries who claimed legal jurisdiction; and, for the most dangerous, transferred to the Department of Defense's control and its detention center at Guantanamo Naval Base, Cuba.

The Evolving *Army Field Manual*

The 1992 version of the *Army Field Manual 34–52, Intelligence Interrogation* (1992), clearly recognized the need to restrain military interrogators from engaging in torture. Prohibited were such things as mock executions; electric shock; infliction of pain; chemically induced psychosis; forcing an individual to stand, sit, or kneel in abnormal stressful positions for prolonged periods of time; food and sleep deprivation; and beatings.

Following the 9/11 attacks, attitudes about interrogations within the Department of Defense shifted. By December 2001, the Pentagon planned the use of several new interrogation techniques with suspected al-Qaeda and Taliban fighters in anticipation of the February 2002 presidential memo, which denied al-Qaeda and the Taliban the protections of the Geneva Conventions and its Common Article 3 and denied them traditional POW status as terrorists. Labeling them stateless *unlawful enemy combatants* permitted the military to use far more aggressive interrogation techniques than those authorized for use against lawful, state-sponsored enemy combatants. Included among the coercive techniques were sensory deprivation, use of stress positions, forced standing for four or more hours, nudity, and using dogs for intimidation. It did not last. By late 2003 to early 2004, and largely in response to internal and external criticism and the shocking images of leaked photos of detainees held in overseas military detention facilities in Iraq—images that shocked America's conscience—the Department of Defense rescinded most of its most controversial techniques.

Within the U.S. Congress, the momentum against the use of harsh coercive techniques against captured terrorist fighters gained traction. In response, the Detainee Treatment Act of 2005 was signed. In turn, the military updated its principal field manual to comply with the act. In September 2006 the Army issued *FM 2–22.3, Human Intelligence Collector Operations*.

This updated *Army Field Manual* restricted the Department of Defense to "18 techniques plus 1," several of which require general officer or higher approval—for example, prolonged isolation or separation. They are shown in the following figure.

Current *Army Field Manual* Interrogation Techniques	
(1) The direct approach	(10) We all know
(2) Incentive approach	(11) File and Dossier approach
(3) Emotional love approach	(12) Establish your identity
(4) Emotional hate response	(13) Repetition
(5) Emotional fear-up approach	(14) Rapid fire
(6) Emotional fear-down approach	(15) Silent treatment
(7) Emotional-pride and ego up approach	(16) Change of scenery
(8) Emotional-pride and ego down approach	(17) Mutt and Jeff
(9) Emotional futility	(18) False flag
	(Plus 1) Separation [considered coercive]

Extracted from *Army Field Manual 2–22.3, Human Intelligence Collector Operations*, Washington, DC, 2006.

Aside from directly questioning a detainee and the use of incentives, permissible psychological ploys include appealing to the detainee's emotions and ego, leading the detainee to believe the interrogator knows more than he or she, and confronting the detainee with false information. A more aggressive tactic includes rapid-fire questioning. Still, others require general officer authorization: "Mutt and Jeff," a phrase adopted from British intelligence and law enforcement, otherwise known as good cop/bad cop technique; false flag, where a detainee is made to believe that he or she is being held by another country known by the detainee for its harsh interrogations with the aim to instill fear and gain cooperation; and separation, where the detainee is socially isolated for extensive periods of time away from colleagues.

Specifically prohibited are any sort of physically coercive contact; threats of force; nudity, sexual acts or posing detainees in sexual positions; hooding except while in transit; beatings, electric shock, burning detainees, or inducing other forms of physical pain; waterboarding; using military dogs to intimidate detainees; mock executions; causing hypothermia; and depriving the detainee of food, water, and needed medical care.

Despite the fanfare that accompanied the publication of the most recent *Army Field Manual* and its endorsement by members of Congress, a 2010 article in *The Journal of Psychiatry & Law* (Evans, Meissner, Brandon et al. 2010) and a follow-on 2012 article in the *Journal of Applied Research in Memory and Cognition* (Evans, Houston, Meissner 2012) suggest that there is little in the way of empirical science to back many of the military's interrogation or interview tactics and techniques. Still, others imply that several of the techniques described in the *Army Field Manual* are likely ineffective, coercive in some instances, and even counterproductive. Most experts agree that further empirical-based research is needed to validate the interrogation techniques or tactics captured within it.

A Major Force for Change

As a lead-up to the need for a sea of change in interrogation doctrine and procedure within the military and intelligence community, Senator John McCain, himself a former POW (1967 to 1973) and the target of harsh interrogations while in custody of the North Vietnamese, voiced his objections in 2005 on the Senate floor against the use of torture by our military and the intelligence community in the battle against terrorism:

> [Although] the enemy we fight has no respect for human life or human rights . . . this isn't about who they are. This is about who we are. These are the values that distinguish us from our enemies, and we can never, never allow our enemies to take those values away. (McCain 2005)

Nine years later, Senator McCain reiterated his concerns over the revelations and findings now tied to the 2014 Senate Select Committee on Intelligence report:

> [T]he so-called "enhanced interrogation techniques" . . . actually damaged our security interests, as well as our reputation as a force for good in the world. . . . I know from personal experience that the abuse of prisoners will produce more bad than good intelligence. I know that victims of torture will offer intentionally misleading information if they think their captors will believe it. I know they will say whatever they think their torturers want them to say if they believe it will stop their suffering. Our enemies act without conscience. We must not. . . . (McCain 2014)

Presidential Executive Order 13491 reflected many of the same views when it was signed by President Barack Obama on January 22, 2009. It will be discussed in the next chapter.

Rights of Persons in Custody

3

At least four amendments in our Constitution, along with several statutes and a number of international treaties signed by the United States, protect persons in custody or detention from mistreatment, including torture, at the hands of abusive interrogators. Quite simply, their aims are to protect a person's human dignity and fundamental human rights—something all interrogators need to keep in mind. More importantly, these collective documents serve as a vital reminder that sticking to our nation's core values is important—on or off the battlefield—and when engaged in law enforcement, military, or intelligence interrogations.

At what point do interrogations violate human dignity? The U.S. Supreme Court has long considered interrogations to violate human dignity if "cruel and unusual" mistreatment "shocks the conscience." Federal courts have also held that, in some cases, such violations of human dignity—"cruel, inhuman, and degrading treatment"—can be implied even absent evidence of any pain or physical injury to the subject. To a far more limited degree, the Courts have also found that foreign terror detainees held overseas in U.S. government detention facilities may receive some protections under the U.S. Constitution, even when located offshore or in foreign territories, if such facilities the U.S. wholly managed by the U.S. military.

Constitutional Provisions

Fifth Amendment

> **Fifth Amendment of the U.S. Constitution**
>
> No person shall be held to answer for a capital, or otherwise infamous crime, unless on a presentment or indictment of a grand jury, except in cases arising in the land or naval forces, or in the militia, when in actual service in time of war or public danger; nor shall any person be subject for the same offense to be twice put in jeopardy of life or limb; nor shall be compelled in any criminal case to be a witness against himself, nor be deprived of life, liberty, or property, without due process of law; nor shall private property be taken for public use, without just compensation.

The Fifth Amendment creates a number of rights relevant to both criminal and civil legal proceedings. In criminal cases, the Fifth Amendment guarantees the right to a grand jury, forbids double jeopardy, and protects against self-incrimination. The right against self-incrimination serves as an important foundation in the *Miranda* ruling. It also requires that due process, commonly interpreted as fairness, be part of any proceeding that denies a citizen life, liberty, or property.

The "due process clause" prohibits intentional acts by federal officials done in the course of their government duties, i.e., under color of law, that are so maliciously offensive to human dignity that they "shock the conscience" and cause unjustifiable harm to a person.

Sixth Amendment

> ### Sixth Amendment of the U.S. Constitution
>
> In all criminal prosecutions, the accused shall enjoy the right to a speedy and public trial, by an impartial jury of the state and district wherein the crime shall have been committed, which district shall have been previously ascertained by law, and to be informed of the nature and cause of the accusation; to be confronted with the witnesses against him; to have compulsory process for obtaining witnesses in his favor, and to have the assistance of counsel for his defense.

The Sixth Amendment guarantees the right to a public trial without unnecessary delay, the right to a lawyer, the right to an impartial jury, and the right to know your accusers and the nature of the charges and evidence against you. It has been most recently tested in a series of cases involving terrorism, but much more often plays a part, for example, in cases that involve jury selection or the protection of witnesses, including victims of sex crimes as well as witnesses in need of protection from retaliation. Along with the Fifth Amendment, the Sixth Amendment right to an attorney took center stage in the *Miranda* ruling.

Eighth Amendment

> ### Eighth Amendment of the U.S. Constitution
>
> Excessive bail shall not be required, nor excessive fines imposed, nor cruel and unusual punishments inflicted.

Certainly the shortest among the amendments in the Constitution and often discussed in the context of the death penalty, the Eighth Amendment prohibits government officials associated with the criminal processes from intentionally resorting to or inflicting "cruel and unusual punishment" that fails to meet "evolving standards of decency" to a convicted criminal or someone held as a pre-trial detainee. The excessive fines clause surfaces, among other places, in cases of criminal forfeiture, for example, when property is seized during a drug raid.

Fourteenth Amendment

> **Fourteenth Amendment (excerpt) of the U.S. Constitution**
>
> Section 1.
>
> All persons born or naturalized in the United States, and subject to the jurisdiction thereof, are citizens of the United States and of the state wherein they reside. No state shall make or enforce any law which shall abridge the privileges or immunities of citizens of the United States; nor shall any state deprive any person of life, liberty, or property, without due process of law; nor deny to any person within its jurisdiction the equal protection of the laws . . . .

The rulings under the Fourteenth Amendment apply to the states and not the federal government. The Fourteenth Amendment offers state residents safeguards against arbitrary denial of life, liberty, or property by their state government. It carries the "equal protection clause" and provides that no state shall deny to any person within its jurisdiction the equal protection of the laws. At the time of its introduction, residents among several states, in some circumstances, had different levels of protections from those offered by the federal government. Another right found in the Fourteenth Amendment, the "due process clause" is the only right stated twice in the Constitution, signaling its importance.

While the Fifth Amendment imposes the due process requirement on the federal government, the Fourteenth Amendment does the same for the states. In this Amendment, the phrase "equality before the law" interprets the "due process clause" to prohibit acts by state government officials in the course of their duties which "shock the conscience;" a ruling we discussed in Chapter 2 under *Rochin versus California* (1952).

International Treaties

Like the system of checks and balances in the U.S. Constitution, the United States has elected to subject itself to international laws and protocols that offer checks on the use of power in times of war and international conflict. Such recognition stemmed in part from the belief that only by binding itself to a system of domestic and international laws that oppose abusive use of power, such as torture, could the United States hope to avoid becoming what it most opposes—a totalitarian regime.

Universal Declaration of Human Rights

The United Nations (UN) General Assembly adopted the Universal Declaration of Human Rights to clarify the rights and fundamental freedoms that member nations were obliged to protect. The Universal Declaration prohibits such things as arbitrary arrest, detention, or exile of persons, as well as torture and cruel or inhuman or degrading treatment. The Universal Declaration is not a treaty and technically not binding on the United States, although a number of its provisions are understood to reflect customary international law. The Universal Declaration does not include an enforcement provision.

Geneva Conventions and Common Article 3

Four Major Treaties of the Geneva Conventions

- The First Geneva Convention protects wounded and sick soldiers on land during war.

- The Second Geneva Convention protects wounded, sick, and shipwrecked military personnel at sea during war.

- The Third Geneva Convention applies to POWs.

- The Fourth Geneva Convention affords protection to civilians, including those in occupied territories.

The Geneva Conventions of 1949 and its four separate treaties, reflected in the above figure, are at the core of international humanitarian law, the body of law that seeks to regulate the conduct of war. Through it, responsible nations seek to protect innocent persons from harm who do not, or no longer, take part in fighting, such as noncombatant civilians, aid workers, children, women, medical personnel, and shipwrecked and wounded soldiers. As of the year 2000, 194 nations agreed to the Conventions, making it largely accepted throughout the globe.

Respect and protection of human life are at the root of the Geneva Conventions. To accomplish it, the Conventions call for punitive criminal trials against nations and leaders who violate its treaties. Such violations are formally called "grave breaches." Those responsible for "grave breaches" are liable for extradition and trial to the International Criminal Court in the The Hague, no matter what nationality they may hold. Among other duties of the signatories to the Conventions are the obligations, vis-a-vis the civilian population, to provide humanitarian relief in territories where they serve as occupying powers; and the duty to permit access to detainees and POWs under their custody or control to the International Committee of the Red Cross.

Common Article 3

Common Article 3 marks a breakthrough in the agreements since it covers, for the first time, situations of noninternational armed conflict or, in other words, conflicts short of general war. According to the International Committee of the Red Cross, 80% of the victims of conflicts since 1945 have been victims of noninternational armed conflict and, typically, such conflicts are often even more cruel and lethal than general international wars. Types of noninternational armed conflicts vary greatly. They include traditional civil wars, internal armed conflicts that spill over into other nations, or internal conflicts in which a third-party government or a multinational force intervenes alongside a legitimate government under attack. These include our experiences in Korea and Vietnam and contemporary conflicts such as present-day Syria, Iraq and Afghanistan.

> ### Common Article 3 for Conflicts Short of International War
>
> In the case of armed conflict not of an international character occurring in the territory of one of the High Contracting Parties, each party to the conflict shall be bound to apply, as a minimum, the following provisions:
>
> (1) Persons taking no active part in the hostilities, including members of armed forces who have laid down their arms and those placed "hors de combat" by sickness, wounds, detention, or any other cause, shall in all circumstances be treated humanely, without any adverse distinction founded on race, colour, religion or faith, sex, birth or wealth, or any other similar criteria.
>
> To this end, the following acts are and shall remain prohibited at any time and in any place whatsoever with respect to the above-mentioned persons:
>
> (a) violence to life and person, in particular murder of all kinds, mutilation, cruel treatment and torture;
>
> (b) taking of hostages;
>
> (c) outrages upon personal dignity, in particular humiliating and degrading treatment;
>
> (d) the passing of sentences and the carrying out of executions without previous judgment pronounced by a regularly constituted court, affording all the judicial guarantees which are recognized as indispensable by civilized peoples.
>
> (2) The wounded and sick shall be collected and cared for.
>
> An impartial humanitarian body, such as the International Committee of the Red Cross, may offer its services to the parties to the conflict. The parties to the conflict should further endeavour to bring into force, by means of special agreements, all or part of the other provisions of the present Convention.
> The application of the preceding provisions shall not affect the legal status of the parties to the conflict.

In many ways, Common Article 3 is like a miniconvention within the Conventions since it contains the essential rules of the Geneva Conventions in a condensed format and makes them applicable to conflicts not of an international character. Among its key provisions, Common Article 3 states that all persons taking place in hostilities "shall in all circumstances be treated humanely" and bans all "violence to life and person," including "cruel treatment and torture" . . . and "outrages upon personal dignity, in particular, humiliating and degrading treatment" at any time and in any place whatsoever.

In instances of both the Geneva Conventions and Common Article 3, the International Committee of the Red Cross is given the right to offer its services to the parties in conflict and may request access to POW internees and protected persons held in detention centers to ensure their humanitarian needs are met. Such humanitarian needs include food, shelter, clothing, medical treatment, personal mail, and recreation.

UN Convention against Torture

The most well known among international agreements prohibiting torture is the *UN Convention against Torture and Other Cruel, Inhuman, or Degrading Treatment or Punishment,* sometimes referred to in some circles as *the Convention* or *CAT* in others. It has more than 140 nations as its signatories and was adopted by the UN General Assembly in 1984. It went into effect on June 26, 1987. The core provisions of the Convention establish a regime for international cooperation in the criminal prosecution of torturers. Each state party to the Convention is required to either prosecute torturers who are found in their territory or permit their extradition to other countries for prosecution.

While a number of prior international agreements and declarations condemned and prohibited torture, the Convention appears to be the first international agreement to actually attempt to define the term. Article 1 of the Convention specifies that torture is understood to mean

> any act by which severe pain or suffering, whether physical or mental, is intentionally inflicted . . . for such purposes as obtaining . . . information or a confession, punishing . . . intimidating or coercing . . . for any reason . . . when such pain or suffering is inflicted by or at the instigation . . . consent or acquiescence of a public official or other person acting in an official capacity. It does not include pain or suffering arising only from, inherent in, or incidental to lawful sanctions.

Importantly, this definition clearly specifies that both physical and mental suffering can constitute torture, and that for such suffering to constitute torture, it must be purposefully inflicted. Additionally, acts of torture covered under the Convention must be committed by someone acting under the "color of law." So, for example, if a private individual is the cause of intense suffering of another, absent the "instigation, consent, or acquiescence" of a public official, such action does not constitute torture for purposes of the Convention. The Convention also requires governments to take effective measures to prevent torture within their borders, and forbids governments from transporting people to any country where there is reason to believe that they will be tortured.

The United States ratified the Convention in 1994. But, it did so with a Senate reservation that (1) the act specifically intended to inflict severe physical or mental pain or suffering; and that (2) the U.S. considers itself bound to prevent cruel, inhuman or degrading treatment or punishment only to the extent that such treatment or punishment is prohibited by the Fifth, Eighth, and Fourteenth Amendments to the U.S. Constitution.

International Covenant on Civil and Political Rights (ICCPR)

Article VII of the ICCPR, ratified by the United States in 1992, prohibits states from subjecting persons "to torture or to cruel, inhuman, or degrading treatment or punishment." The Human Rights Committee, the monitoring body of the ICCPR, has interpreted this prohibition to prevent governments from exposing "individuals to the danger of torture or cruel, inhuman or degrading treatment or punishment upon return to another country by way of their extradition, expulsion or refoulement." (Refoulement, by the way, is the forcible return of refugees or asylum seekers to a country where they are liable to be subjected to persecution.)

Although the Human Rights Committee is charged with monitoring the compliance of parties with the ICCPR, its opinions are not binding law. The U.S. ratification of the ICCPR was contingent upon the inclusion of a reservation that the treaty's substantive obligations were not self-executing (i.e., they require domestic-implementing legislation in order for courts to enforce them). The United States also declared that it considered Article VII binding to the extent that "cruel, inhuman or degrading treatment or punishment" (prohibited by ICCPR Article VII) means the cruel and unusual treatment or punishment prohibited by the Fifth, Eighth, and Fourteenth Amendments to the Constitution of the United States. The United States has not yet enacted laws or regulations to comply with the Human Rights Committee's position that ICCPR Article VII prohibits the transfer of persons to countries where they would likely face torture or cruel, inhuman, or degrading treatment.

Istanbul Protocol

The 1999 Istanbul Protocol, also called *The Manual on the Effective Investigation and Documentation of Torture and Other Cruel, Inhuman or Degrading Treatment or Punishment*, is a nonbinding set of international guidelines which encourage governments to document incidents of torture and other forms of ill-treatment and to punish those responsible in a prompt and impartial manner. Among its provisions, the Istanbul Protocol warns governments, physicians, and lawyers investigating incidences that "the absence of physical evidence should not be construed to suggest that torture did not occur, since such acts of violence against persons frequently leave no marks or permanent scars."

U.S. Laws, Statutes, and Executive Orders

Torture Victims Protection Act (TVPA)

The TVPA is a statute that allows for the filing of civil suits in the United States against individuals who, acting in an official capacity of a foreign government, committed torture or extrajudicial killings. The statute requires the plaintiff to show that he or she exhausted attempts to petition the courts where the event took place, if possible, before seeking the help of U.S. courts.

In 1992, Sister Dianna Ortiz was the first to file a case under the act, in a civil action against former general and Defense Minister Héctor Gramajo of Guatemala, contending that he was responsible for her abduction, rape, and torture by military forces in Guatemala in November 1989. A federal court in Massachusetts ruled in her favor, awarding her $5 million in damages in 1995. And, the TVPA has also been used by both foreign national and U.S. victims of terrorism to sue foreign states that had been designated by the United States as sponsors of terrorism, such as Iran, if the plaintiff can show that his or her injuries were caused by the state's support of a terrorist organization.

War Crimes Act (WCA)—18 U.S.C. § 2441

Federal law 18 United States Code (U.S.C.) § 2441 is known as the War Crimes Act. Fully in effect from 1997 to 2006, the WCA broadly criminalized all violations of Common Article 3 of the Geneva Conventions. The WCA applies to acts committed "inside or outside the United States" in any circumstance "where the person committing such war crime or the victim of such war crime is a member of the Armed Forces of the United States or a national of the United States."

In 2006, the Military Commissions Act (MCA) narrowed the definition of what are "war crimes" by asserting only "grave breaches" of Common Article 3 would constitute war crimes and citing the nine specified acts listed in the WCA. They are

1. *Torture.* The act of a person who commits, or conspires or attempts to commit, an act specifically intended to inflict severe physical or mental pain or suffering (other than pain or suffering incidental to lawful sanctions) upon another person within his custody or physical control for the purpose of obtaining information or a confession, punishment, intimidation, coercion, or any reason based on discrimination of any kind.

2. *Cruel or inhuman treatment.* The act of a person who commits, or conspires or attempts to commit, an act intended to inflict severe or serious physical or mental pain or suffering (other than pain or suffering incidental to lawful sanctions), including serious physical abuse, upon another within his custody or control.

3. *Performing biological experiments.* The act of a person who subjects, or conspires or attempts to subject, one or more persons within his

custody or physical control to biological experiments without a legitimate medical or dental purpose and in so doing endangers the body or health of such person or persons.

4. *Murder.* The act of a person who intentionally kills, or conspires or attempts to kill, or kills whether intentionally or unintentionally in the course of committing any other offense under this subsection, one or more persons taking no active part in the hostilities, including those placed out of combat by sickness, wounds, detention, or any other cause.

5. *Mutilation or maiming.* The act of a person who intentionally injures, or conspires or attempts to injure, or injures whether intentionally or unintentionally in the course of committing any other offense under this subsection, one or more persons taking no active part in the hostilities, including those placed out of combat by sickness, wounds, detention, or any other cause, by disfiguring the person or persons by any mutilation thereof or by permanently disabling any member, limb, or organ of his body, without any legitimate medical or dental purpose.

6. *Intentionally causing serious bodily injury.* The act of a person who intentionally causes, or conspires or attempts to cause, serious bodily injury to one or more persons, including lawful combatants, in violation of the law of war.

7. *Rape.* The act of a person who forcibly or with coercion or threat of force wrongfully invades, or conspires or attempts to invade, the body of a person by penetrating, however slightly, the anal or genital opening of the victim with any part of the body of the accused, or with any foreign object.

8. *Sexual assault or abuse.* The act of a person who forcibly or with coercion or threat of force engages, or conspires or attempts to engage, in sexual contact with one or more persons, or causes, or conspires or attempts to cause, one or more persons to engage in sexual contact.

9. *Taking hostages.* The act of a person who, having knowingly seized or detained one or more persons, threatens to kill, injure, or continue to detain such person or persons with the intent of compelling any nation, person other than the hostage, or group of persons to act or refrain from acting as an explicit or implicit condition for the safety or release of such person or persons.

Federal Torture Statute—18 U.S.C. § 2340–2340B

In response to the 1987 UN Convention Against Torture, Congress did not enact new domestic laws to criminalize acts of torture committed within the jurisdiction of the United States. It was presumed that such acts would be covered by existing applicable federal and state statutes. However, it did add Chapter 113C to the United States Criminal Code (Federal Torture Statute, 18 U.S.C. § 2340–2340B), which criminalizes acts of torture that occur outside the United States to implement its treaty obligations under the Convention.

The Torture Act criminalizes acts of torture committed by a government official or representative acting "under color of law" and specifically intending to inflict severe physical or mental pain or suffering upon a person within his custody or control under the following four elements of proof:

1. The act took place outside of the United States.
2. The act was performed under color of law.
3. The victim was under the defendant's custody or physical control.
4. The act was intended to inflict severe physical or mental pain or suffering.

The statute defines "severe mental pain or suffering" as prolonged mental harm caused by or resulting from (1) the intentional infliction or threatened infliction of severe physical pain or suffering; (2) the administration or threatened administration of mind-altering substances; (3) the threat of imminent death; or (4) the threat that another will be imminently subjected to any of the above three acts to coerce and influence the principal subject.

Detainee Treatment Act (DTA)

Popularly called the *McCain Amendment*, the DTA, which Congress passed in 2005, asserts that "no person in the custody or under the physical control of the United States government, regardless of nationality or physical location, shall be subject to torture or cruel, inhuman, or degrading treatment or punishment." Among other things, the DTA contains provisions that

- Requires all members of the U.S. military to employ United States *Army Field Manual* guidelines while interrogating detainees;
- Prohibits the "cruel, inhuman and degrading treatment or punishment" of persons held in detention, custody, or control of Department of Defense and in its holding facilities;
- Removed the federal courts' jurisdiction over detainees wishing to challenge the legality of their detention, stating that "no court, justice or judge shall have jurisdiction to hear or consider" applications on behalf of Guantanamo detainees; and
- Provides legal defense to U.S. personnel in any civil or criminal action brought against them on account of their "good-faith" participation in the authorized interrogation of suspected foreign terrorists.

Within the DTA, prohibitions against "cruel, inhuman or degrading treatment or punishment" is the same as in the UN Convention Against Torture and is interpreted to mean "the cruel, unusual and inhumane treatment or punishment" prohibited by the Fifth, Eighth, and Fourteenth Amendments to the U.S. Constitution.

Military Commissions Act (MCA)

In response to the restrictive provisions of the 1996 WCA and the 2005 DTA, which the Bush administration claimed impeded U.S. government interrogations in its war against terrorism, and the *Hamdan* ruling, which applied Common Article 3 to the war with al-Qaeda and held that military tribunals or commissions to try terrorists needed Congressional legislation, the White House encouraged Congress to pass the MCA. It did in 2006. This act narrows interpretations of the DTA and violations of Common Article 3 to the nine specified "grave breaches" listed in the WCA, previously discussed.

Within the MCA, torture is defined as "an act specifically intended to inflict severe physical or mental pain or suffering (other than pain or suffering incidental to lawful sanctions) upon another person within his custody or physical control for the purpose of obtaining information or a confession, punishment, intimidation, coercion, or any reason based on discrimination of any kind." Cruel or inhuman treatment is defined in the MCA as "an act intended to inflict severe or serious physical or mental pain or suffering including serious physical abuse, upon another within his custody or control."

The MCA also reestablished military tribunals or commissions, suspended under the *Hamdan* ruling, to prosecute select terror defendants held in Guantanamo rather than offer them access to U.S. courts. The MCA was highly controversial at the time of its passage. Civil rights advocates claimed that it suspended detainee rights of habeas corpus and due process, violated the U.S. Constitution, and ignored still other provisions in the Geneva Conventions.

In 2008, and on review of the MCA, the U.S. Supreme Court held in *Boumediene versus Bush* (2008) that a terrorist detainee held in Guantanamo had the right to petition federal courts under *writ of habeas corpus*, but that such challenges do not guarantee release and upheld continuing detention even if the petitioner is no longer a threat. Moreover, the Court reaffirmed the use of military tribunals or commissions to prosecute Guantanamo defendants, at the government's discretion, for their war crimes. In response to the Court's rulings, and an accommodation to the judicial challenge, the MCA was amended in 2009 to offer some additional Constitutional protections for defendants (see https://www.aclu.org/).

Executive Order 13491

Two days after taking office on January 20, 2009, President Obama issued Executive Order 13491 under the title *Ensuring Lawful Interrogations*. In its opening paragraph, the new Presidential order revoked former President Bush's Executive Order 13440 of July 20, 2007, which had offered al-Qaeda and Taliban captives only limited protections of the Geneva Conventions and Common Article 3. Instead, this new executive order affirmed Common Article 3 of the Geneva Convention, the Federal Torture Statute, and the Detainee Treatment Act as the standards for the humane treatment of detainees held in U.S. government detention facilities.

Next, in a direct rebuke of the enhanced interrogation program, President Obama's order revoked "all directives, orders, and regulations inconsistent with this order and issued to or by the Central Intelligence Agency from September 11, 2001 to January 20, 2009 concerning detention or the interrogation of detained individuals." Black sites were ordered closed. Additionally, with publication of the President's executive order, the CIA officially terminated its rendition, interrogation, and detention program.

The executive order then set other compliance standards for our nation's interrogation program. It declared *Army Field Manual 2–22.3* (2006), *Human Intelligence Collector Operations*, as the operative interrogation directive for the Department of Defense and the entire intelligence community. In doing so, the executive order now restricts the intelligence community and any others performing interrogations inside Department of Defense internment or holding facilities to techniques and tactics contained within the *Army Field Manual.*

In sharp contrast to the restrictions placed on the general intelligence community, the Federal Bureau of Investigations and other federal law enforcement agencies received an exemption when performing interrogations outside of Department of Defense internment facilities to existing "authorized, non-coercive techniques of interrogation that are designed to elicit voluntary statements and do not involve the use of force, threats, or promises." The "techniques" were never specified.

As a matter of emphasis, the executive order reiterated the prohibition against

- Torture, as defined under Federal Torture Statute (18 U.S.C. § 2340);
- Cruel, inhuman, and degrading treatment, as defined under the DTA and MCA;
- Any activities subject to criminal penalties under the WCA, such as murder, rape, and mutilation;
- Willful and outrageous acts of personal abuse done for the purpose of humiliating or degrading the individual in a manner so serious that any reasonable person would deem them beyond the bounds of

human decency—sexually indecent acts, threatening the person with sexual mutilation, or using the individual as a human shield; and

- Acts intended to denigrate the religion, religious practices, or religious objects of the individual.

Further, the executive order directed the U.S. Attorney General to create a Special Interagency Task Force on Interrogation and Transfer Policies. Among its responsibilities, the Special Interagency Task Force was tasked to

- Evaluate the adequacy of *Army Field Manual* and its interrogation techniques for use by agencies outside of the Department of Defense and to recommend any other additional or different guidance for such agencies;
- Establish a scientific research program for interrogation in order to "study the comparative effectiveness of interrogation approaches and techniques with the goal of identifying existing techniques that are the most effective and developing new lawful techniques to improve intelligence interrogations"; and
- Review the practices of transferring individuals to other nations under the rendition program.

On August 24, 2009, the Special Interagency Task Force released its findings and concluded

- That the *Army Field Manual* "provides appropriate guidance for military interrogators and that no additional or different guidance was necessary for other agencies" (DOJ 2009). It did not further amplify.
- That with regard to the rendition program, the Task Force mandated U.S. transfer practices included injecting the U.S. State Department to monitor the treatment of transferred persons to nations receiving detainees.

For our nation's most dangerous terror captives, the Attorney General approved the creation of the High-Value Detainee Interrogation Group (HIG). By design, the HIG is to bring together the most effective and experienced interrogators from across the intelligence community, the Department of Defense, and law enforcement; and its main role would be intelligence gathering. Yet the Special Interagency Task Force guidance also provides the option of preserving information to be used in potential criminal investigations and prosecutions. Interrogations of high-value terrorists would be performed by mobile teams of experienced interrogators, analysts, subject matter experts, and linguists. Among its roles, the HIG would also develop and publish a set of best practices for conducting interrogations.

In a follow-up to his executive order and in a White House press release on April 16, 2009, President Obama stated that his administration was not interested in prosecuting current and former intelligence officers who carried out interrogations based on the Department of Justice's legal reasoning prior to the issuance of his 2009 executive order:

> This is a time for reflection, not retribution. I respect the strong views and emotions that these issues evoke. We have been through a dark and painful chapter in our history. But at a time of great challenges and disturbing disunity, nothing will be gained by spending our time and energy laying blame for the past. Our national greatness is embedded in America's ability to right its course in concert with our core values, and to move forward with confidence. That is why we must resist the forces that divide us, and instead come together on behalf of our common future. (White House 2009)

Challenges Yet Ahead

The case law rulings and interpretations of the Fifth, Sixth, Eighth, and Fourteenth Amendments are continuously evolving for both criminal suspects held in custody by police within the United States and for foreign terror suspects and enemy combatants held by our military in overseas U.S. government detention facilities. All are open to evolving legal interpretations and policy debates.

In general, the courts have determined the following types of acts are prohibited under these Amendments:

- Handcuffing an individual to a post or wall in a standing or stressful position for an excessive period of time.
- Maintaining temperatures and ventilation systems in detention facilities that fail to meet reasonable levels of comfort.
- Prolonged interrogations over an extended period, including interrogations of a duration that might not seem unreasonable but becomes such when evaluated in the totality of the circumstances.
- Intentionally causing serious bodily harm, maiming, and injury involving a substantial risk of death; or causing extreme physical pain, disfigurement, or the loss or impairment of the function of a body member, organ, or mental faculty.
- Beatings, sexual assaults, and rape.

While it might seem obvious to most of us that the methods highlighted above amount to "cruel, inhuman, or degrading treatment or punishment," a leading number of congressional lawmakers—led by Senators John McCain of Arizona and Dianne Feinstein of California—wanted to avoid any ambiguity when it came to interrogations in conflict or war zones. Together, the two Senators rallied bipartisan support in 2015 to add an amendment to the 2016 Defense Appropriations Act. Titled *Limitations on Interrogation Techniques*, and short-named the *McCain–Feinstein Amendment*, it cements into law key features of President Obama's Executive Order 13491. The aims were clear: to close any misinterpretations of the laws against torture and deny the opportunity for future presidents to loosen the reins.

This amendment now broadens the mandate found in the DTA of 2005. Now, "all" government agencies must rely on the *Army Field Manual* when engaged in detainee interrogations, further solidifying the aims of President Obama's Executive Order. The amendment stipulates that any person in custody or under control of the United States or detained in a U.S. facility in any armed conflict can be interrogated using only the techniques in the *Army Field Manual*. Federal law enforcement, as an exception, would continue to use previously approved, noncoercive techniques.

Also tied to the amendment is the requirement for the Department of Defense to review and update the *Army Field Manual*, no later than one year of the amendment's enactment and at least once every three years thereafter, capturing relevant "evidence-based, best practices" that do not rely on physical violence or threats of force and which elicit "reliable" and "voluntary" statements. In support of transparency, the amendment mandates that the *Army Field Manual* continue as an openly available and accessible unclassified publication. Moreover, the amendment asserts that all agencies of the government engaged in overseas operations must provide the International Red Cross with access to detainees held in their custody or control.

On Being Human

4

An infinite number of variables are at play inside the interrogation room that impact the subject and the interrogator. The most impactful among them are the dynamics of being human. Your understanding of how being human influences the suspect or detainee gives you a powerful vantage point to better understand the person sitting before you—on a human level—and what it may take to influence the subject to cooperate with questioning and, ultimately, steer the interrogation to a satisfactory outcome.

Understanding Memory

As pointed out in a government-sponsored Intelligence Science Board study, interrogators need a sound understanding of how memory works and how it sometimes fails us—how it perceives, stores, and retrieves information (Intelligence Interviewing 2009). Without this basic knowledge, interrogators may misinterpret or even contaminate the information inside the subject's memory, fail to help the subject with memory recall, or fail to discern truth from lies. And, while the human brain still largely remains a great mystery, recent breakthroughs in cognitive science are teaching us more than we have ever known about the human mind and memory.

Many people believe that the human mind acts like a video recorder, capturing all experiences exactly as they occur and storing them in a database— our memory—until retrieved. Such a model overestimates the capacity of the human brain. Consequently, when a suspect or detainee fails to provide a full picture or claims to have no memory of the topic, the tendency is to interpret the faulty memory to an uncooperative, evasive, or deceptive subject. Typically, the common response of interrogators is to ratchet up the psychological pressure on the subject with tactics that further elevate stress and tension, which may further exacerbate memory recall abilities (Educing Information 2006). Knowing what we now know about stress on memory recall, a better alternative strategy might be to try working calmly with the subject to help the person remember the information sought. But to do so requires a shift in existing interrogation paradigms.

Shown in the following figure are examples of some factors that may neg-atively influence or alter memory recall and the ability of a person to accu-rately perceive, store, and retrieve information.

Major Influence on Memory Recall
• Fragility of memory recall over time
• Contaminated or compromised knowledge based on unconscious influence of the questioner
• A false confession based on psychological vulnerability to police or interrogator inducement
• No knowledge of events or persons
• Effects of stress on an individual's behavior and memory recall
• Deliberate acts of lying, deceit, and omission or obfuscation

Other Factors Influencing Memory

An infinite number of other factors also influence memory and outcomes inside the interrogation room. Here are some obvious ones.

Gisting

Our memories favor gisting (broad concepts) over details. So while the capac-ity of human memory for gist is quite good, our memory for associative details may fail us, particularly over time or in high-stress situations, and is vulnerable to suggestion. It seems that in a highly charged life-altering event, we also expe-rience a sort of tunnel vision retaining the most vivid memories of the central or core event while often discarding peripheral information. Such implications about our memories are important, especially when an interrogator is trying to help someone recall details for court testimony in a criminal case or when we are debriefing a victim or witness after a terror attack.

Reality Mapping

Errors in reality mapping mean that a person may retain a memory, but forget or misattribute the origin of that memory. For example, a mem-ory may have originated in a daydream, a conversation with a friend, a story read or seen in a movie. In trying to recall the memory, the per-son may misattribute the original source to the wrong one. This explains why the memory may be real in the mind's eye, but a real memory is not necessarily accurate. Too often, as we previously just discussed in the section "Gisting," it seems that we are poor judges of the accuracy of our own memories. For example, an individual may remember the overall content of a conversation at a meeting, but at the same time may make several errors with regard to who said what and the order in which people spoke.

Stress

Stress, even at moderate levels, may impair memory recall in subjects—especially during interrogations—or in eyewitnesses (Loftus 2011). A textbook example of this comes from the annals of Northwestern University's School of Law near Chicago where Professor Fred Inbau—the respected lifelong associate of John E. Reid—taught criminal justice for 32 years. During one of his classes, an armed robber burst in and mugged Inbau in the middle of a lecture on policing. After the robber fled with his briefcase, Inbau asked the class to describe his attacker. An abbreviated synopsis of student observations is captured below. The results were startling.

> Some said the robber was fat; others said thin. Some said the robber wore glasses; others said he didn't. Some said he was short about 5 feet 6 inches; others as tall as 6 feet 6 inches tall. Some said the robber's hair was jet black; others said bleached blond or it just might have been mousy brown. Some said the robber wore a denim shirt and blue jeans; others a leather jacket and brown corduroys. (*The Economist*, June 11, 1998)

By the way, the entire event was staged. Inbau, the professor, was a skeptic on the reliability of eyewitnesses and sought to persuade his students to put their faith in hard forensic evidence over witness statements.

Passage of Time

We know memories decay over time without use, but not all memories decay at the same rate. Additionally, once recovered, information apparently becomes easier to retrieve the second time around, thus slowing the decay. Once remembered, the repetition of a story or event may have an impact on the retrieval of other ancillary information to the point where the story will slightly change with each retelling, as new details are recalled and retrieved. Along these same lines, the more meaningful and personally relevant an event is to the person, the more easily the person will retrieve the core information. If carefully done, providing cues or prompting with partial detail may help the person recall information. But be careful. Priming memory with hints and cues may also corrupt the accuracy of that information, even in fully cooperative subjects.

Suggestibility and Memory Distortion

The study of suggestibility is to understand that, under certain conditions, "leading" questions are likely to have a powerful influence on memory recall in witnesses or victims. Consequently, interrogators need to keep in mind the form, the content, and the manner in which their questions are asked and framed. Inadvertently, a questioner may influence vulnerable persons to suggestion and, therefore, to false recollections. And, once a person has recalled information falsely, it may be difficult for that person to let go of the false memory and distinguish it from a real one.

Along the same lines of suggestibility, memory distortion occurs when postevent information contaminates the recall of events, say a crime or an accident. Again, subjects may unconsciously simply repeat what they have learned from a neighbor, friend, or from the news media. As with suggestibility, once inaccurate postevent information is recalled during an earlier retrieval attempt, it increases the likelihood that the same incorrect information will be recalled in a subsequent retrieval opportunity (Loftus 2011).

Situational Dynamics

Such factors may include the circumstances and the time of day of the arrest and the interrogation. More often than not, for example, executing an arrest early in the morning and suddenly waking someone up from sleep is disorienting and may weaken a subject's ability to resist and cope with the subsequent questioning. Or, simply the shock of capture might influence a subject to cooperate.

Physical and Emotional Isolation

Abject feelings of loneliness and separation from family and friends are commonly the first emotions anyone behind bars experiences. Moreover, many interrogation manuals emphasize isolating the subject from external influences that might obstruct his or her willingness to confess, tell the truth, or answer questions.

Fear

Fear involves the desire to avoid harm and uncertainty and, in either instance, can be a powerful motivator. Going through an arrest and being confined behind bars are clearly stressful events, especially for the first-time offender. With rare exceptions, people change when they enter the interrogation room and are brought under custody and placed in detention. They frequently lose their identity and confidence. Loyalties change; priorities change (Interview with Michael Koubi: Israeli Interrogator 2004). A person's imagination may go wild as well. Such uncertainty frequently raises fear levels: fear of being locked up with strangers; fear of the consequences for lying to the interrogator; and, if guilty, fear tied to the consequences of a confession. Such emotions may serve as powerful precursors for either truth-telling or deceit.

Guilt, Shame, and Humiliation

Guilt, shame, and humiliation serve as three emotions that frequently influence an interrogation. Shame is often perceived by a subject as a degrading, humiliating experience. It often accompanies a sense of exposure. In contrast, guilt is associated with some real or imagined past wrongdoing that is inconsistent with the person's values and standards. While feelings of guilt may serve to motivate some to confess, feelings of shame and humiliation have the opposite effect, often hardening the person against confession.

As an example of this, read what Marine Sergeant Andrew Tahmooressi said in an abridged excerpt from a television interview shortly after his release from a Mexican prison. He spent over 200 days behind bars in 2014 under suspicion of gunrunning charges to which he was never tried. Tahmooressi spoke in vivid detail about his experience and "exposure" in the aftermath of an escape attempt and how his prison guards reacted:

> I was very afraid. I felt like it would be the last night of my life right there. That these guys were going to kill me. That these guys were going to brutally kill me. . . . They [the guards] began hitting me and I thought to myself "bring it on." I expected it. Then they stripped me of my clothes; forced me to stand in the dark naked and cold and tied me to a pole for 8 or 9 hours overnight. Then they brought me into a small dark cell, partially clothed me and had me lie on a bed facing upright, restrained with one arm and leg on opposite bed posts; and left me that way in full view of hardened prisoners walking past my cell. . . . So, I'm like some kind of animal in a cage here . . . like I don't even have life in me. . . . I was totally exposed, humiliated, and felt completely vulnerable. (Fox News Interview with Andrew Tahmooressi 2014)

Physiological Factors

Upon initial arrest, subjects commonly experience heightened physiological arousal, which includes increased heart rate and blood pressure, irregular respiration, and above normal perspiration. These physiological changes occur because subjects are typically apprehensive, worried, and frightened. Such elevated physiological factors may affect a subject's health in general and, more importantly, memory and recall abilities. Typically, once a subject confesses, there are sharp reductions in physiological arousal because of greater short-term certainty about the immediate future. Arousal and fear may then return to heightened levels just before trial or a preliminary hearing because of uncertainties tied to the pending prosecution.

Perceptions

A subject's behavior during an interrogation is often influenced more by personal perceptions about what is happening rather than by the actual behavior of the interrogator or actual events. For instance, a guilty subject's perceptions about the strength of evidence in possession of the police often serve as a strong motivator either to confess or to continue deceptive lies. For most people, a guilty subject is far more likely to confess if he or she perceives that the incriminating evidence is strong. Or, if the subject perceives that the interrogator is experienced and doggedly persistent, the person may simply confess to avoid even tougher questioning. On the other hand, if a guilty subject believes that the investigator lacks sufficient evidence or lacks adequate experience, a hardened suspect or detainee may simply continue to lie or deceive rather than self-incriminate and open up about the information in his or her possession.

Physical Setting

The physical setting of the interrogation room and the detention center also play an important role in the success or failure of influencing a subject to talk. For an interrogator, it is worth considering how to create an environment that facilitates effective communication exchanges and getting to the truth rather than establishing physical barriers or distractions that may inhibit effective communication. The research suggests that it is easier to persuasively influence people who find themselves in a conducive environment that resonates in positive ways. Keep extraneous people, noise, and voices to a minimum. Make sure the room's temperature is set at a comfortable level. And pay attention to strange odors that may serve as a distraction. Other suggestions for setting up the interrogation room are reflected in the following figure.

Suggestions for Interrogation Rooms	
• Make it conducive to eliciting responses.	• Remove logos or pictures from walls.
• Select plain, simple decor, neutral off-white wall paint with good lighting.	• Use unobtrusive A/V recording devices and hidden cameras that do not distract—these are preferred to one-way windows.
• Keep noise to a minimum, providing privacy without any distractions.	• The interrogator and the subject should be separated by about 4 to 5 ft and should directly face each other without any other object between them to avoid any sort of physical barrier.
• Interrogators should dress conservatively, preferably in business attire; most guidelines suggest no uniforms.	

Bias

Important to the interrogation process is the need to understand our biases and their impact on us. Our biases wield a tremendous influence not only on the interrogator but, equally as well, on the suspect or detainee and the evolving interpersonal dynamics between the two. And, this influence is not always negative. Biases can exert both positive and negative influences among people—on our attitudes, our perceptions and beliefs, and treatment of each other. Whether in a law enforcement or intelligence context, the important thing to remember is that our biases can skew objectivity in an interview or interrogation, the direction an investigation takes, the ability to establish rapport, the tone and types of questions asked, and the outcome of an interrogation or even an entire investigation.

By the time most interrogators enter the interrogation room, they are fully formed adults with a history of family baggage, decades of group and cultural influences, and a lifetime of professional and personal experiences behind them. Most law enforcement officers have climbed the ranks from patrol officer to detective before conducting interrogations as part of their investigative duties. Similarly, most intelligence professionals managed a successful career before leading them to a midcareer decision to train as interrogators and debriefers. Among their counterparts, only military interrogators possess a full-time career track and are trained as interrogators upon entry to the armed forces. And, don't forget, suspects and detainees are likewise influenced by their childhood and life experiences. Over the course of all their lives, these people—interrogators and suspects or detainees—have collected millions of memories and such thoughts wield powerful conscious and unconscious influences.

Some of our memories are fairly obvious but most are stored in the recesses of our brains. The circumstances we encounter can trigger those memories, often in ways that we are not fully aware. Some we readily acknowledge and are called *conscious biases*; others may not be as obvious and are hidden away from our conscious thoughts but just as influential. We call these *unconscious biases*. During the interrogation process, conscious and unconscious biases may lead us down the wrong path, prejudicing our judgments of probable guilt or innocence in others and the value of any information we elicit from them simply based on biased stereotypes. In psychology, this is referred to as "confirmation bias."

Can we eliminate the hold that conscious and unconscious biases have over us? Perhaps not as much as we might hope, especially that of unconscious bias. But, by exercising self-awareness and acknowledging the existence of bias and the influence it may have over our lives, especially inside the interrogation room, are big steps in mitigating and marginalizing their influence. In the process, acknowledging bias may prompt us to take greater steps to see the suspect or detainee on a human level (Ross 2014).

Infliction of Pain and Threats

Keep in mind that deliberately inflicting pain or even the threat of pain or death against a subject is unlawful by our laws, the U.S. Constitution, and several international treaties. Importantly, too, any information gained through such actions is generally inadmissible in a court of law and may prove unreliable from an intelligence context. Reports about physical abuse of POWs in China during the Second World War and the Korean War demonstrated that such tactics were often ineffective in gaining consistently reliable, accurate information. Subjects were known to say just about anything, including falsely incriminating themselves, just to make the pain stop. Moreover, pain can negatively affect the tenor of the relationship—rapport—between the interrogator and the subject and certainly decreases the likelihood of voluntary cooperation. In most cases, those interrogators who revert to such tactics will certainly be seen as bullies.

In a bizarre twist, and in other wartime observations, some POWs actually became accustomed to pain during interrogations to the point that it served no useful purpose. Rather than getting the detainee to talk and become submissive, excessively harsh coercive tactics over an extended period actually influenced the resolve of some detainees to resist the brutality of their handlers and interrogators. Such was one of the themes in the movie and in the book *Unbroken* (2010) by Laura Hillenbrand, which tells the inspirational story of former Olympian and World War II POW survivor Louie Zamperini, who served as a bombardier in the Army Air Corps in the Pacific theater. Here is a stylized account from the movie that emphasizes this point:

> On May 27, 1943, while on a search mission for a downed aircrew, mechanical problems caused Zamperini's plane to crash into the Pacific Ocean 850 miles south of Oahu, Hawaii. Adrift in a rubber raft nearly 50 days, the three surviving airmen subsisted on what little rainwater and fish they could catch until the Japanese Navy discovered him, and his only surviving companion, near the Marshall Islands. Separated from his companion, Zamperini was initially held at Kwajalein Atoll for several weeks in a small, confined cage-like cell. Fearful, isolated, and absent human interaction, Zamperini acted out in bizarre ways, often screaming and slamming his body against the sides of his cage. Forty days later, he was transferred to Ofuna Interrogation Center near Yokohama, an undeclared internment facility for high-value detainees. Later, he is transferred yet again to Tokyo's Omori POW camp and eventually to Naoetsu POW camp, where he stayed until August 1945 and the war's end. At both of these last two internment camps, Zamperini encountered the brutal and sadistic Japanese Corporal Mutsuhiro Watanabe, who took on the role of Zamperini's tormentor, subjecting the airman to almost daily inhuman treatment and abusive beatings, yet reinforcing the unyielding resolve within Zamperini to survive. In a major scene near the end of the movie we see Zamperini struggling to stand tall holding a wooden beam over his head. Recognizing his inability to defeat him, Watanabe fell to his knees in tears. Zamperini survived his mistreatment and the war, unbowed and unbroken through sheer determination and courage.

Interpersonal and Intrapersonal Dynamics

Whether in a law enforcement or intelligence context, the interrogation process can be effectively distilled to its underlying dynamics: "a controlled exchange of information on both an interpersonal and an intrapersonal level" (Educing Information 2006).

The Science of Rapport

At the start of an interrogation, it is hard to know what is motivating the person sitting across from you. Is he or she willing to cooperate with you or not? Will he or she be truthful? One proven way to help achieve your aims in an interrogation is by establishing rapport with the subject.

The word *rapport* comes from the French *raport*, meaning "to report." The earliest use of the term referred to the act of bringing back information and connecting one party to another. A *rapporter* was one who connected or formed a relationship between two parties through the act of reporting some type of information. *Reporter*, the occupational identifier of a person tied to the news media, is a derivative of the word. The term *rapport* has evolved to mean a "special bond" between two persons, in this case between the interrogator and the subject.

Building rapport is an important factor in almost all successful interrogations and starts the moment you make eye contact with the subject and continues throughout all your interactions. It involves the interrogator creating the perception of a constructive experience for the subject on an interpersonal or psychological level (Tickle-Degnen & Rosenthal 1990).

> The dynamic is intensely interpersonal; it is therefore all the more necessary to strike a counter-balance by an attitude which the subject clearly recognizes as essentially fair and objective. (*KUBARK Manual* 1963)

If the subject perceives that he or she will be treated fairly and learns to trust and respect the interrogator, then, perhaps, he or she may be more responsive to the interrogator's questions. Anecdotal evidence suggests that a failure to build rapport early in the interrogation process is one of the leading causes of unsuccessful interrogations (Walsh & Bull 2012).

One way to help in the process of rapport-building is to create in the subject's mind a "perception of similarity" between the interrogator and the subject. According to a 2014 *Harvard Business Review* article by Northeastern University Professor David DeSteno, "The Simplest Way to Build Trust," there is nothing complicated about it. All that is required to increase a person's willingness to cooperate is to find and emphasize something—anything— that will cause the subject to see a common link or special bond with the interrogator. It could be as small as an article of clothing, pendant, or wristband that both share; or the ability to leverage common cultural or linguistic identities; or a shared meal, snack, or beverage. Or it might be simply a lighthearted discussion about a favorite sport or athlete before beginning the serious questioning.

Choose Your Words, Demeanor, and Tenor Wisely

Ever wonder why some people are better interrogators than others? Perhaps, it is because they are just more effective and strategic at communicating and interacting with their targets. They think through what they say before they say it. Their interrogation successes are likely high because they have a better read of the subject and develop the ability to construct a more persuasive message that resonates on a human level.

Research shows that interrogators who think through what they say, understand the power of their words, and speak in a calm, steady, and clear tone of voice have a greater chance of achieving their desired outcomes. Such interrogators possess the ability to deliver persuasive and influential messages that may ultimately move an uncooperative subject to the goal of responding to questions with useful and reliable information in support of either intelligence requirements or an open police investigation (Heuback 2009).

Research suggests that those who are verbally aggressive or abusive lower their chances of persuasively influencing the listener. Sure, there are times when raising one's voice might be effective. Yet no one enjoys being put down and called names. No one enjoys being made to feel inferior and less than human. No one enjoys being humiliated. Such interrogators and their abusive language are more frequently perceived as less effective in achieving successful interrogation outcomes. Verbally abusive interrogators make people feel uncomfortable and rely on character attacks, competence attacks, insults, teasing, ridicule, profanity, etc. The targets of their abuse not only will resent them, but also will likely resist their efforts of persuasion and influence (Delia 2008).

On another point, it is important that the interrogator be respected by the subject and one of the most effective ways of accomplishing that is by controlling your demeanor, the tone of your voice, and the words you use. The selection of words you use and how you deliver them do matter. Those interrogators who understand this have an advantage over other interrogators. Moreover, as you will read next, gaining perceived credibility, trust, and respect in the eyes of the subject further supports your efforts at rapport-building and persuasion.

Six Key Elements of Interpersonal Dynamics

Why are we attracted to some people over others? Robert Cialdini explains it in his book *Influence: The Psychology of Persuasion*, first published in 1984 in support of the advertising and marketing industry. His insights into interpersonal dynamics and the power behind influence and persuasion focus our attention on six key elements. All of us should familiarize ourselves with them, not only to help explain their influence over interpersonal dynamics inside the interrogation room, but also as a tool to help managers and leaders as well. Let us now explore these six key elements (see the following figure)—slightly modified to accommodate the interrogation process.

Major Influencers on Interpersonal Dynamics	
1. Trust/respect	4. Commitment/consistency
2. Authority	5. Social validation
3. Reciprocity	6. Scarcity

Adapted from Cialdini, R. B., *Influence—The Psychology of Persuasion*, William Morrow, New York, NY, 1984.

Trust and Respect

People prefer to say yes to those they trust, respect, and perceive in positive ways. Remember, the suspect or detainee need not like you, but they should believe they can trust and respect you. In general, people feel comfortable with those they trust and respect, those that behave in a positive manner, and those they believe are objective and fair.

Authority

Most cultures respect requests from authority figures. We are also more likely to be influenced by messages from a person whom we perceive in respectful terms—those that use titles such as "detective," "senior sergeant," or "doctor." Such titles and personas elevate the status of the interrogator in the eyes of the subject and may help contribute to influencing a subject's willingness to talk. So, select your persona carefully.

Reciprocity

There is a powerful—often unspoken—social norm of reciprocity, variously known as "give and take," or a "two-way street." The philosophy behind this theory is that most people are more likely to respond positively to requests for information from someone who has first provided a benefit, incentive, or favor to them—whether tangible or intangible—rather than from someone who has not. Such a benefit might mean a warm meal or the ability to call their loved ones. When a person begins to feel the pull to reciprocate, a suspect or detainee may have often little to offer the interrogator other than the information he holds.

Commitment and Consistency

People want to see themselves—and be seen by others—as fulfilling their promises and commitments. People are more likely to cooperate or be influenced in a particular direction if a request is consistent with a previous message or is for the better good. Another example of this is for an interrogator to discuss with the subject that a particular request for information does not violate his or her prior commitments to others and that, perhaps, responding to the request would serve to help family or friends.

Social Validation

Social validation is especially influential when these two elements are present: (1) uncertainty—a person who is unsure of his or her surroundings and in an ambiguous situation is more likely to seek social validation—and (2) similarity—people are more inclined to follow the lead of others in social settings who seem similar to themselves. Using this principle, a detainee or a suspect is more likely to provide information if he or she believes "others" in his or her cohort, such as a criminal gang, have already done so. This works most powerfully when the others are similar in various ways (e.g., age, race, interests, and socioeconomic status) to the subject.

Scarcity

Under the scarcity principle, something that is easily attainable is not nearly as desirable as something scarce or rare—such as a phone call to loved ones. An interrogator might offer a conditional incentive for information that is available only if the subject decides within a specified time frame, after which "all deals are off." To a subject in confinement, the diminishing availability of the incentive serves as a potent motivating force.

Five Core Needs of Intrapersonal Dynamics

Every one of us has emotional needs and these needs possess a powerful intrapersonal influence over the way we think and behave. According to Roger Fisher and Daniel Shapiro's 2005 book *Beyond Reason: Using Emotions as You Negotiate*, these needs are distilled into five major influences highlighted in the following figure.

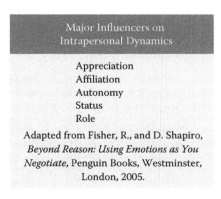

Major Influencers on
Intrapersonal Dynamics

Appreciation
Affiliation
Autonomy
Status
Role

Adapted from Fisher, R., and D. Shapiro,
*Beyond Reason: Using Emotions as You
Negotiate*, Penguin Books, Westminster,
London, 2005.

The degree of influence these five core needs have over people varies from person to person. In other words, people have stronger needs in some areas than others. For instance, one subject may have a stronger desire to feel respected, while another may have a stronger need to feel a sense of companionship. Moreover, all five core concerns are in constant flux and must be continuously evaluated for the person or target group you are trying to influence; their degree of influence changing over time. From an interrogator's vantage point, understanding these five core concerns provides an insightful opportunity to understand the subject on an intrapersonal level. By doing so, you will have another valuable tool toward rapport-building, influencing the subject, and achieving a successful outcome in the interrogation.

Appreciation
People often feel appreciated when they believe someone seeks to understand their point of view. Appreciation may be communicated verbally, such as by the use of a respectful language, or by the action of offering something special to the subject, perhaps as simple as a cup of coffee (which may also lead to some reciprocity). By doing so, an interrogator shows the detainee or suspect that he or she empathizes with many of the subject's experiences, thoughts, and feelings.

Affiliation
Feeling connected to others can be emotionally comforting. Rapport can result more easily and quickly when people believe in the perception that they have something in common. Here, the interrogator might seek to uncover common links with the subject, perhaps by discussing family, work experiences, religious backgrounds, sports, or hobbies. Emphasizing the shared nature of their common experiences increases the subject's relationship to the interrogator in positive ways, which the interrogator can then leverage as a tool during questioning.

Autonomy
The need for autonomy varies across cultures and among individuals. However, almost all people wish to feel they possess at least some control over their lives. A person who has a strong need for autonomy is likely to find detention particularly tough, and might likely become even more resentful if constantly told what to think, what to talk about, and how to behave—in addition to being told what to wear and when to eat and sleep. Since control is built into a detention setting, the interrogator may be able to mitigate resistance by creating the perception that the subject is being offered some small area of control over their lives—to stand or to sit, whether to eat alone privately or with a group—in exchange for cooperation. At times, it might

even be helpful to permit the detainee or suspect to control the direction of a conversation. As one master interrogator observed: "From my point of view, the subject who seeks to take control by asking questions can be quite useful to a savvy interviewer—one can learn a great deal from the questions that are asked" (Intelligence Interviewing 2009).

Status

Almost all individuals enjoy the feeling that they are respected and viewed as important. Regardless of the interrogator's private opinion of the subject, acknowledging a subject's former status—as a professional person, a leader, a parent, etc.—may provide another way for an interrogator to gain some persuasive leverage. Such recognition elevates the subject's sense of self-importance while elevating positive perceptions of the interrogator.

Role

People play many roles in life and may find it hard to give up these roles, particularly while detained behind bars. If a subject is viewed and treated only as a radical jihadist or a hardened criminal, he or she will likely persist in such behaviors and belief systems. An interrogator might reduce the subject's resistance by drawing out other roles that the subject has played—perhaps as an educator, a student, a father, a husband, a theologian, or a member of a sports team.

Put These Concepts into Action

Taken as a collective group, and put into action during an interrogation, these conceptual theories potentially provide us with powerful and exploitable points of leverage and influence. They explain the interpersonal and intrapersonal dynamics that influence interrogations.

Quite simply, positive words and actions, objectivity and fairness, and perceptions of empathy are more quickly associated with people we feel comfortable with and want to communicate with, while those who we perceive in negative terms by their harsh language or abusive actions turn us off. These same perceptions—good or bad—are experienced among those we interrogate.

So keep these concepts in mind as we enter Chapter 5 and learn to develop tailored interrogation strategies.

The Interrogation Cycle

5

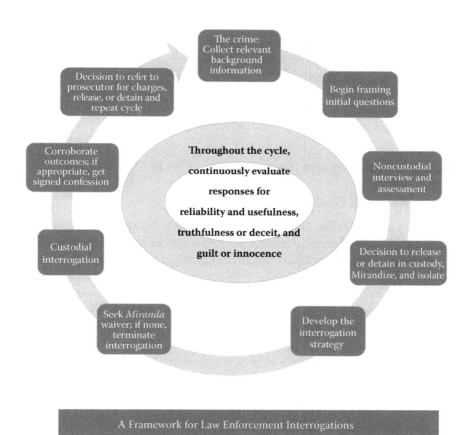

The crime: Collect relevant background information

Begin framing initial questions

Decision to refer to prosecutor for charges, release, or detain and repeat cycle

Noncustodial interview and assessment

Corroborate outcomes; if appropriate, get signed confession

Throughout the cycle, continuously evaluate responses for reliability and usefulness, truthfulness or deceit, and guilt or innocence

Decision to release or detain in custody, Mirandize, and isolate

Custodial interrogation

Seek *Miranda* waiver; if none, terminate interrogation

Develop the interrogation strategy

A Framework for Law Enforcement Interrogations

The law enforcement interrogation cycle portrayed above captures the major steps and decision points in a baseline interrogation of a criminal suspect. Each step around the circle dependent on the step preceding it. The inner circle emphasizes that throughout the cycle, the interrogators are continuously evaluating the suspect's responses for reliability and usefulness, truthfulness or deceit, and cues to guilt or innocence. A conceptual framework for an intelligence-related interrogation will also be addressed later in this chapter. In most cases, however, the framework for law enforcement interrogations provides an insightful tool for the intelligence community as well, less the need to Mirandize an alien enemy combatant captured outside the United States and its territories.

Unlike classic legacy methodologies, this contemporary model advocates spending extra time and energy in four steps often overlooked and not routinely emphasized: (1) researching, collecting, and analyzing relevant background information on the crime and suspect; (2) framing initial questions leading up to the noncustodial interview and custodial interrogation; (3) crafting a flexible interrogation strategy tailored to the subject; and (4) corroborating postinterrogation outcomes—particularly a confession or an admission—with the oversight of senior managers. Investing sufficient time and energy in corroborating and evaluating postinterrogation outcomes aims to limit the influence of confirmation bias on the part of the interrogator, limits false confessions from entering the judicial system, and injects stronger accountability into the overall process.

The Law Enforcement Interrogation Cycle

Collect Relevant Background Information

All authorities agree that a solid analysis of relevant background information and research about the crime are essential to a successful interrogation. Such analysis helps set the overall direction of the investigation and may offer insights into the motives behind the event and the persons of interest or the suspect.

Relevant background information includes such baseline reporting as crime scene photos or video; medical investigator's and examiner's results; forensics and DNA testing; ballistic analysis; and statements from victims, witnesses, informants, and co-conspirators. Do not forget, as well, to evaluate possible cultural dynamics at play which may have influenced the subject. Also, as part of this preparatory stage in a criminal investigation, your research into the major statutory elements of proof for the crime under investigation may help you develop initial questions when the time comes for the noncustodial interview and custodial interrogation.

Knowing how to ask the right type of questions is perhaps one of the most important, but often overlooked, skill sets of an investigator. According to Fisher and Geiselman (1992), the recognized experts of cognitive interviews, eliciting as much information as possible from victims and witnesses is considered one of the best predictors of solving a crime. Yet their research demonstrates that most law enforcement officers lack effective interviewing skills and, consequently, overlook key pieces of information.

As explained in Fisher and Geiselman's paper, *The Cognitive Interview Method of Conducting Police Interviews: Eliciting Extensive Information and Promoting Therapeutic Jurisprudence* (2010), most investigative interviews of victims and witnesses follow a similar pattern. They open with a series of questions aimed at collecting demographics from the witness or victim and then move on to the perfunctory open-ended "What happened?" In a matter of a few seconds into the respondent's narrative explanation, the interviewer typically cuts off the person and unleashes a barrage of close-ended, short-answer questions: "How old was the robber?" "Was he white or black?" "Was he tall or short?" "Did he have a weapon?" "How much money was stolen?" This line of questions continues until the investigator exhausts his or her arsenal of crime-relevant questions. At the end, the interview terminates with the pro forma "Is there anything else?"

Fisher and Geiselman (2010) assert that the typical background interview is too heavily dominated by the investigative interviewer asking far too many questions; forcing the witness or victim to play an ancillary or subordinate role. They claim that too many witnesses or victims merely "help out" in the process—giving short answers to questions that are far too specific, close-ended, or leading. Additionally, most victims and witnesses are often discouraged by investigators from volunteering details that do not relate to the immediate question; in the process, chains of thought are frequently interrupted and disrupted. Emoting emotions are typically discouraged, too, despite the fact that in many instances the person just experienced a traumatic life event. Instead, the sequencing of the interview and the questions too often follow a perfunctory written checklist and, quite often, are designed to confirm the interviewer's hypothesis. Under such frameworks, typical police questioning practices limit the amount of information witnesses provide and increase chances of inaccurate responses. In summary, classic questioning methodologies encourage people to withhold unsolicited, yet important, information; emphasize abbreviated answers to close-ended questions; depersonalize the question-and-answer process; emotionally handcuff the victim and witnesses; and, in the end, make them feel more like a suspect than as part of the investigative process and a team member to the investigation.

Instead, Fisher and Geiselman (2010) suggest that investigators need to be better listeners and refrain from asking too many questions—so many questions, in fact, that investigators typically overwhelm the respondent. Broad open-ended questions are far more effective. Investigators can further help witnesses and victims by enhancing their memory recall of a crime event by considering the following suggestions:

- Invest sufficient time and effort at the outset of an interview to develop meaningful rapport and trust with the victim and the witness. Remember, in most instances, these people just experienced a life-changing event and may have to talk about potentially embarrassing circumstances to an investigator who, in most cases, is a complete stranger to them.

- Permit the victim and witnesses to fully explore, describe, and recall their emotions and feelings at the time of the original crime event.
- Capitalize on broad open-ended questions, not inject a barrage of close-ended questions, or cutoff explanations while witnesses or victims are searching their memories.
- Suggest that respondents close their eyes to enhance concentration and memory recall—provided, of course, sufficient rapport and trust are established.
- Tailor questions to the respondent's most vivid experiences or mental images, e.g., the weapon, the suspect's clothes, or the facial description, about the crime event instead of relying on a fixed checklist of questions.
- Avoid confusing the respondent by cutting off the narration and asking questions about the color of the suspect's hair at the moment he or she is talking about the weapon.
- Defer control of the interview to the victim or witness since it is their thoughts and memories that should direct the course of the questioning rather than subordinate them to the interviewer's needs or assumptions. "I'm interested in what you have to say. What you saw? What you experienced?"
- Enhance recollection by asking the respondents to describe the event or crime scene several times within the interview and arrange to interview the victim or witness on more than one occasion to capitalize on the recall of new details, which is common days after the first interview terminated.
- Instruct the victim or witness to refrain from guessing, and tell them that it is okay to say, "I don't know."
- Permit the victim or witness to narrate using nonverbal language, such as drawing or sketch, using model figurines, or even acting out the event just as he or she experienced and observed it.
- Arrange for non-English-speaking victims or witnesses to record their narratives in their native language with a reliable and vetted interpreter to assist with follow-up questioning.

A Cognitive-Based Interview Methodology

Within the field of interviewing, the cognitive interview reflects a multidisciplinary approach backed up by empirical research from cognitive psychology. The protocol has been extensively examined in laboratory and field studies in a number of countries and has employed the use of empirically driven techniques shown to increase the elicitation and retrieval of accurate information, especially by victims and witnesses. Quite simply, the cognitive interview leads to better memory recall of events, whether for law enforcement or intelligence, compared to traditional interview methods (McLeod 2010). As an example, the cognitive interview commonly includes the following steps.

Step One: Recreate Feelings or Perceptions of the Event   Here, the interviewer might ask the victim or witness to recall the dominant memory of the event under investigation and then follow up with questions that elicit sensory experiences of the incident: "What did you feel?" "What did you hear?" "What were you touching or holding?" Such questions are designed to stimulate memories from among different neural pathways—emotional, auditory, kinesthetic, etc.

Step Two: Recollect Event in Sequence   During this point in the cognitive interview, the victim or witness is asked to recall the event in chronological sequence in a free flow of memory without any interruption on the part of the interviewer. Following the retelling of the event, the interviewer would then frame follow-up questions relying on key words or phrases from the subject's own words: "OK, Sammy, you told me that you were in the store standing at the counter. What did you observe about the person in front of you?" "What did the person look like?" Such questions are designed to stimulate secondary memories based on the subject's recall of his or her primary memory at the crime scene.

Step Three: Reverse the Order of the Recall of Events   Here, the subject is asked to recall events in reverse order. The aims of such a process seek to validate the previous retelling and sequence of events at the crime scene or, quite possibly, uncover deception on the part of the subject.

Step Four: Recall from Another Person's Perspective   Ask the subject to describe the incident from another person's perspective, such as that of the victim, further stimulating memories in the subject.

Step Five: Recall the Event by Sketching a Map   This technique aims to validate what the victim or witness tells the interviewer against actual recollections of the crime scene, validating or disproving storylines of the event while stimulating alternative memory pathways.

Frame Initial Questions

As with victims and witnesses, the quality of the answers you get from a suspect or detainee depends on the quality of the question asked. To create and ask the right questions, you need to know something behind framing questions. This is especially true for the noncustodial interview, which hinges on the ability of an interrogator to ask meaningful questions of the subject. So avoid suggestive questions that can lead people to incorporate inaccuracies in their responses. The subsequent recall of incorrect information can be partially offset by not introducing misinformation or contamination through the use of poorly framed questions.

Think through, too, what your questions may reveal to the subject in the way of expectations and perceptions. Whether intentional or not, a question may provide the recipient insights about what you may expect him or her to know or not know and what you, the interrogator, may know or not know. Perceptive subjects may likely use these insights to their advantage.

To avoid poorly framed suggestive and contaminated questions, brainstorm your proposed questions ahead of time with the assistance of another interrogator. Together, you should explore the range of the information gaps you need filled and explore the range of possible assumptions underlying the suspected person's involvement or knowledge of the act or event. Importantly, too, by participating in such creative thinking processes before you enter the room, you will limit the influence of bias in your questioning. Remember, too, that knowing the specific elements of proof for the particular category of crime under investigation will help you focus and frame your questions to the crime.

In planning your interrogatives or questions for the noncustodial or pre-interrogation interview, rely on open-ended questions, which require the subject to amplify answers in narrative-type responses, rather than on close-ended questions, which typically produce short yes/no responses. And remember these six key questions: "who?" "what?" "when?" "where?" "how?" and "why?" These six questions provide you the basic building blocks to use in asking your questions whether in a criminal or intelligence context.

By the way, here are some general suggestions from experts, such as the authors Robert Royal and Steven Schutt in their seminal book *The Gentle Art of Interviewing and Interrogation* (1976), on the fundamentals of good question design:

- Make the questions short and confined to one topic—avoid compound questions combining more than one question in a question.
- Make the questions clear and easily understood.
- Avoid the use of frightening or superrealistic words, such as *confession, murder, forger, dope addict, terrorist,* and *embezzler.* Use milder terms.

- Use precise questions. A precise question is one that calls for a specific or an exact answer. It limits the requested answer to a definite item of information.
- Use discerning questions. Discerning questions are questions designed to produce information directly bearing on the matter under discussion.
- Design your questions to accommodate the cognitive intellect, the education level, and the linguistic ability of the person under questioning.
- Rehearse your questions in advance especially if using an interpreter.

In further context to open-ended questions, here is the type of open-ended question to avoid: "Why did you use gasoline to destroy the victim's body?" Here, the interrogator runs the risk of undermining objectivity and accuracy of the information received. The question is leading and offers the subject too much insight into the investigation. In contrast, a solid open-ended question might ask, "What happened to the body?" Here, the subject is asked to answer based on his or her knowledge and memory, without the benefit of clues contained in the question. Along the same lines, avoid negative questions such as "Did you go to the gym or not?" The response here may not only confuse you but also the subject. Whether the subject responds with "yes" or "no," it is unclear what you are asking the subject.

And make sure to exercise self-discipline and self-awareness inside the interrogation room. Listen to the subject's responses without overt reactions and constant interruptions. By allowing the subject to tell his or her story without interruption, an interrogator aims to achieve basic objectivity and help in the process of rapport-building.

Dillon's Five-Question Methodology

A technique worth knowing is Dillon's (1990) *five-question technique.* Originally designed for schoolteachers and academic counselors, Dillon's methodology proposes five separate types of question to ask in sequential order.

Initial Opening Questions   Initial opening questions are used at the start of the interview and designed to get the subject talking. These should be simple yes/no questions that are easy to answer and are not about the crime or event.

Free Narrative Questions   Here, the interviewer names a topic tied to the investigation and asks the subject to tell what he or she knows about it, giving the subject sufficient time to describe a topic in his own words while the interviewer listens without interrupting.

Direct Questions   A direct question is a follow-up on the narrative-type responses by asking about specific items while avoiding value-laden terms such as *murder, explosion,* and *rape.* The interrogator should rank his questions (a) from the general to the specific and (b) from the known to the unknown.

Cross-Questions   These questions are designed to check and verify one answer against another, delving into problematic (i.e., contradictory or ambiguous) answers. The subject is asked to repeat his or her statements to questions asked in different ways and in no special order.

Review Questions   These questions are used to confirm previous answers, repeating the information and asking, "Is that correct?" and "What else?"

At the closing of any interview or interrogation, most experts suggest simply casually chatting with the subject. Such small talk may lead to an unguarded statement from the suspect or detainee that contains new information because the subject perceives that the questioning is over and reverts to a more relaxed state. Regardless of the questioning technique you use, always remember to repetitively ask for clarification such as "Tell me more to make sure I understand." And do not forget to use this as the final question during all your interviews or interrogations: "Do you have any information relevant to this investigation that we have not discussed?"

Noncustodial Interview and Assessment

The noncustodial interview is normally the first sit-down meeting between the interrogator and the subject. This important step in the interrogation cycle provides the opportunity to assess the likelihood of knowledge or culpability and guilt of the subject to the event under investigation, to validate holding the subject as a legitimate suspect or detainee, and to understand the subject as a person and get a handle on what makes him or her tick. This includes the subject's motivations, psyche, and emotional vulnerabilities; an opportunity to evaluate the subject's willingness to cooperate and his or her degree of resistance; and to uncover short- and long-term interpersonal and intrapersonal motivational influences.

Underlying this step in the interrogation cycle are these important points: (1) find out what the subject is willing to talk about; (2) find out what the subject is hesitant to disclose; and (3) find out what the subject is uncomfortable talking about.

Typically, noncustodial interviews are structured around a two-part process. In the first part of the interview, the interrogator or investigator is using the opportunity to gather personal or demographic information with relevance to the investigation from the subject. In the process of collecting this neutral data, the interrogator is able to evaluate and determine the subject's normative behavior patterns and general anxiety level. Simultaneously, during this early stage of the interview, the interrogator is also establishing rapport and assessing the subject's cognitive skills, communication and language abilities, anxiety levels, and physical and mental health.

In the second part of the interview, the investigator or interrogator commonly asks preliminary investigative-type questions. Remember that in a law enforcement noncustodial interview, the suspect is not yet under arrest or formally charged with a crime. Consequently, the police are permitted to question the subjects in a noncustodial setting absent the reading of *Miranda* rights.

Provided there is no spontaneous confession or admission at this stage, the results of the noncustodial interview logically feed into the next step in the interrogation cycle.

Decision to Release or Detain in Custody, Mirandize, and Isolate

Based on the outcome of the noncustodial interview, subjects may be released or further detained and placed in custody. If detained and placed in custody, U.S. citizens and residents are always read the *Miranda* warning and informed of their rights to an attorney.

There is one important exception to the reading of the *Miranda* warning. It is labeled the *public safety exception* and it was admittedly exercised by the police and the Federal Bureau of Investigation in 2013 with the surviving Boston bomber Dzhokhar Tsarnaev, a naturalized U.S. citizen. Under the *public safety exception*, law enforcement officers making an arrest need not read suspects their *Miranda* rights upon capture if doing so impedes law enforcement efforts to uncover imminent threats to public safety or identify future terrorist plans. The exception is necessitated by the belief that should such a suspect receive the *Miranda* warning too early after capture, the suspect might simply invoke the right against self-incrimination and stop talking, crippling further intelligence collection efforts (Wright 2013).

The decision to detain in custody and Mirandize is sometimes accompanied by the act to isolate the subject before starting the custodial interrogation. Isolation has two basic aims. First, emotional and physical isolation helps to elevate additional anxiety, insecurity, fear, and self-doubt in the subject caused by the uncertainty of what will happen next. Indirectly, it is a routine form of psychologically softening up the subject for the custodial interrogation. Second, although the suspect may exercise his or her right to an attorney at this point, the isolation helps to shut off the subject from other outside influences, such as co-conspirators or family members, who may influence the subject's storyline. Provided that it is not excessive, such as over many days, and deliberately done to punish the subject—isolation is an accepted practice in a law enforcement context. Additionally, the time spent in isolation provides the interrogator the opportunity to prepare for the next step in the interrogation cycle—developing the interrogation strategy.

Develop Your Interrogation Strategy

Once you are convinced that an individual should be questioned in a custodial setting, you need to develop a flexible interrogation strategy tailored to the suspect or detainee before stepping foot inside the interrogation room. While crafting it, keep in mind that your goal is to get an unwilling person suspected of guilt to cooperate and confess to a crime in a law enforcement context or reveal what he or she knows—the extent of their knowledge—in an intelligence context. So how do we tailor a strategy to the individual?

Such a strategy requires some tough decisions and thinking about

- the success or failure at the initial rapport-building and the likelihood of the suspect's cooperation or resistance and, if in a law enforcement context, agreeing to a *Miranda* waiver;
- relevant reevaluation and identification of knowledge and gaps about the crime or event;
- review of previous personality-based assessments about the suspect, which may have identified exploitable vulnerabilities—feelings, beliefs, or perceptions about his or her circumstances and interpersonal and intrapersonal dynamics at play;
- relevant topics which were deliberately avoided by the subject in previous discussions; or the need to seek additional clarity;
- the severity of the crime and, if any, the urgency of the present circumstances; and
- the authorized tactics and techniques available to you as tools to achieve cooperation.

As a preparatory step in developing the strategy, you should also identify the right team members to assist in the interrogation. Such team members may include an assisting investigator or interrogator, a forensic psychologist, a linguist-interpreter, a technical subject-matter expert, and, if needed, a person familiar with the subject's cultural nuances. Other variables to inject into this planning step may include the need to decide on the time and place for the interrogation, the review of unresolved information gaps, and getting someone to help with audiovisual recording equipment for the interrogation.

No one strategy or technique will prove effective with all subjects. While selective tactics and techniques are important, keep in mind that they are not ends in themselves. They are tools used by the interrogator to mitigate resistance and persuasively influence cooperation during questioning. More importantly, it is the strength of the interpersonal relationship between the subject and the interrogator—the rapport—that largely determines the outcome of an interrogation and the willingness of the subject to cooperate with questioning. Understanding the concept of acceptable rationalization (see the following figure) in your planning process may also help.

> ### Acceptable Rationalization
>
> One technique to help you match the right approach to a subject is to keep in mind the concept of acceptable rationalization. By doing so, you are helping the subject save face by crafting the right rationalization or acceptable excuse to cooperate. This concept theorizes that many uncooperative subjects in custodial interrogations feel the growing internal stress that results from wanting simultaneously to divulge and conceal, called the *compliance–resistance dilemma*. To escape from this tension, the subject may grasp at any face-saving reason to cooperate. Your job as the interrogator is to help the subject find the right one.
>
> Modified from Intelligence Science Board, *Educing Information: Interrogation: Science and Art (Phase I)*, National Defense Intelligence College Press, Washington, DC, 2006.

Another aspect of strategy planning is to identify alternative tactics and line of questioning you intend to use with the suspect should your first approach fail. Whatever the tactics you adopt, build flexibility into your strategy and be prepared to respond with agility inside the interrogation room. Understanding the concept of sensory acuity (see the following figure) enables you to plan for both—flexibility and agility—during the execution phase of your strategy.

When Three's Not a Crowd

Existing interrogation models emphasize the need to establish a sense of
complete privacy in the interrogation room between the subject and the
interrogator. The same logic is echoed by the Department of Defense in its
current guidance to interrogators which states that relying on tandem interrogators may have negative consequences and make it "more difficult to
establish rapport" (*Army Field Manual 2–22.3* 2006). Supporting that underlying assumption is the fact that the predominant research on interrogations
has been done largely from an individual interrogator's perspective, not from
the perspective of a two-person interrogation team (Driskell, Blickensderfer
and Salas 2013). In other words, "three's a crowd" inside the interrogation
room. Yet, as we will discuss and demonstrate below, such legacy beliefs may
not reflect what really goes on inside today's interrogation room.

So is it better to have two interrogators in the room or a single interrogator? Which is the better choice? Research scientist Tripp Driskell, formerly
with the University of Central Florida, and his associates examined the possible negative effects of a third person inside the interrogation room (Driskell
and Driskell 2013). The study compared law enforcement interrogations in
which one interrogator was present to interrogations in which two interrogators were present and evaluated the impact on rapport and outcomes.
Results showed no significant difference by having an additional interrogator
present. More so, Driskell's research suggests that a two-person interrogation team is preferable and able to capitalize better on group dynamics and

teamwork which may, in turn, enhance the outcomes of an interrogation. Additionally, the gains achieved from "harnessing the power of the team" may lead to new strategies and approaches to enhance the information gathering aims of interrogations.

Seek the *Miranda* Waiver

Since 1966, U.S. law enforcement investigators have been required to read criminal suspects their *Miranda* rights and seek a voluntary waiver from them before proceeding with the custodial interview or interrogation phase. Should the suspect decide to waive *Miranda*, the investigator may then move forward with the custodial interrogation. Without the waiver, the court may consider the interrogation coerced and the information inadmissible.

The Custodial Interrogation

Despite the large number of interrogation manuals and methodologies on the market, common police interrogation practices within the interrogation room still largely remain a mystery to the general public. What emerges from the 2007 survey of 631 law enforcement officers by Kassin, Leo, Meissner et al. (2007) is a reliable baseline in contemporary police practices—the first self-reported survey ever conducted involving such a large number of law enforcement officers.

The survey depicts that the typical interrogation almost always begins with (1) isolating the suspect away from family and friends, (2) placing him or her in a small private room, (3) identifying contradictions or holes in the suspect's account, and (4) establishing rapport with the suspect in order to gain his or her trust. Should the interrogation intensify, tactics may include (5) confronting the suspect with evidence of his or her guilt and (6) appealing to the suspect's ego and self-interest. Somewhat less frequently, interrogations sometimes include (7) offering the suspect sympathy, moral justifications, and excuses, (8) interrupting the suspect's denials and objections, (9) implying and/or pretending to have independent evidence of guilt, (10) minimizing the moral seriousness of the offense, and (11) appealing to the suspect's religion or personal conscience. On rare occasions, interrogations may include (12) showing the suspect photographs of the crime scene and victim. An underlying presumption of guilt drives the entire process (Kassin, Leo, Meissner et al. 2007). The following figure summarizes and highlights the top 12 techniques relied on by the 631 law enforcement respondents to the 2007 survey.

Commonly Practiced Police Interrogation Tactics (with the % of respondents who claimed to use the tactic routinely)	
• Isolating suspect from family and friends (66%)	• Offering the suspect sympathy, moral justifications, and excuses (13%)
• Conducting the interrogation in a small, private room (42%)	• Interrupting the suspect's denials and objections (13%)
• Identifying contradictions in the suspect's story (41%)	• Implying or pretending to have independent evidence of guilt (7%)
• Establishing rapport and gaining the suspect's trust (32%)	• Minimizing the moral seriousness of the offense (29%)
• Confronting the suspect with evidence of his guilt (22%)	• Appealing to the suspect's religion or conscience (5%)
• Appealing to the suspect's self-interests (11%)	• Showing the suspect photographs of the crime scene and the victim (3%)

Based on Kassin, S. M., R. A. Leo, C. A. Meissner, K. D. Richman, L. H. Colwell, A. M. Leach, and D. La Fon, *Police Interviewing and Interrogation: A Self-Report Survey of Police Practices and Beliefs*, American Psychology–Law Society/Division 41 of the American Psychological Association, 2007.

Legacy Interrogation Tactics and Techniques

In both law enforcement and intelligence, the widely recognized doctrine for interrogators is to rely on the least intrusive, least coercive technique or tactic during an interrogation. Yet, in practice, most legacy interrogation models or methodologies are just the opposite, typically hostile and confrontational. Such strategies reflect a presumptive and confident belief in the subject's guilt in a criminal case or knowledge, in an intelligence context, as an unquestionable fact. Moreover, relying on such logic, many interrogators still believe that innocent persons quite simply would not find themselves inside an interrogation room. Consequently, the traditional focus of law enforcement questioning is often on why the subject committed the act instead of if he or she did it, and dismiss narratives from the subject that amount to claims of innocence.

Additionally, short of physical abuse and torture, the issue of which legacy tactics are coercive and noncoercive remains a matter of debate among U.S. courts and their jurisdictions. However, the trends increasingly consider many of the classic tactics as unethical, coercive in some instances, and highly manipulative or exploitive. In general, the tactics in the following figure have been frequently interpreted as coercive by judges and the courts in criminal cases.

Police Tactics Judged Coercive
• Failing to read the *Miranda* warning or offering the waiver
• Causing pain by aggressive physical manhandling of the suspect
• Failure to offer medical assistance to a subject in physical or psychological pain
• Threats of physical or psychological harm
• Explicit promises of leniency in exchange for an admission of guilt
• Denying the subject essential necessities—food, water, or toilet access
• Unrelenting and hostile questioning over an excessively extended period of time

Adapted from Leo, R. A., *From Coercion to Deception: The Changing Nature of Police Interrogation in America*, University of California, 1992, also published in *Crime, Law and Social Change*, 18, 1–2, 35–59, September 1992.

Classic legacy tactics and techniques taught to police include direct confrontation, theme development, developing details, alternative questioning technique, falsifying evidence, invoking guilt and responsibility, manipulative role-playing, and implying promises. By relying on these aggressive influence strategies and tactics, investigators and interrogators are taught to deceptively manipulate the way a subject feels, thinks, and behaves in ways he or she might otherwise not and in ways that advance the interrogator's underlying assumptions about the subject's guilt or knowledge.

The Direct Confrontation   *Direct confrontation* normally occurs right up front in most traditional interrogation models and basically says to a suspect—"I know you did it, you know you did it, just admit it, and we can move on." Clearly, this approach is accusatory in tone, emotionally charged, and based on the assumption that the subject is guilty. If this fails and the suspect resists, an interrogator's next option is commonly to rely on what is termed the tactic of *theme development*.

Theme Development   Theme development is generally the second technique or tactic used by law enforcement officers following a direct confrontation. Theme development occurs in one of three ways—through *rationalization, projection of blame, and minimization or maximization*. Rationalization is where the interrogator makes the crime seem socially acceptable and even reasonable given the circumstance. For example, investigators may rationalize a bank robbery by telling the suspect that given the state of the economy, other people are making the same decision because of their financial situations. The second kind of theme development is projection of blame which aims to transfer blame to someone or something else entirely—such as the victim or society. For example, in a rape case the interrogator might suggest that perhaps the suspect would not have raped the woman had the victim dressed more conservatively. Some argue that leading subjects to project blame on external factors and escape moral culpability for their criminal actions is deceptive since they create the implication that the subject is not responsible for their actions. The third way a theme is developed is through the use of minimization or maximization. The police may exercise minimization or maximization by either withholding (minimizing) or exaggerating (maximizing) the evidentiary evidence in their possession. They may, for example, tell a suspect that a murder victim is still alive, hoping that this knowledge will compel the subject to talk. Or the police may exaggerate the seriousness of the crime—overstating the amount of money stolen—so that the subject feels compelled to confess to a smaller role in the crime. Or a police officer may tell the subject that they are investigating a minor crime when, in fact, they are really investigating a more serious one. Theme development can be an effective communication strategy because it utilizes justifications for the crimes in hope that the suspect will process and accept them and, in doing so, confess.

Developing Details   A follow-on tactic to theme development is *developing details*, which arises immediately after the suspect makes the first verbal signs of an incriminating statement or admission of guilt—the "OK! I did it" statement. Now, the interrogator withdraws a bit from the intensity of the interrogation and begins to modify his or her communication style to a more empathetic tone. Instead of dominating the conversation, the interrogator now starts to ask nonleading, more open-ended questions. For example, the interrogator may begin asking the suspect to clarify his or her response and then ask why he or she committed the crime and let the suspect tell his or her version of events. This allows the suspect to give a detailed explanation for the crime, ideally leading to a full confession.

Alternative Questioning Technique Another tactic in the law enforcement inventory is the *alternative questioning technique*. The key here is to present the suspect with a choice between two possible explanations for why the crime was committed—one choice more socially or morally attractive or justifiable than the other. For example, in a case involving theft, the suspect is asked, "Did you take the money because you needed it for bills or for drugs?" In logic, this is also referred to as a *false dilemma* and it is an effective tactic because one (or more) of these reasons may account for the rationale behind the crime. If the suspect accepts either one of these explanations, he or she is admitting his or her guilt. In some cases, a suspect may voluntarily offer a third possibility, which, again, serves as an admittance of guilt.

Falsifying Evidence Courts have routinely permitted police to confront a suspect with *false evidence* of guilt. Basically, this strategy has five separate possible tactics. One is to falsely inform the subject that an accomplice has identified him or her. Another is to falsely state that existing physical evidence—such as fingerprints, bloodstains, or hair samples—confirms the subject's guilt. Yet another is to falsely assert that an eyewitness or the victim identified the subject as the perpetrator. One other ploy is to have a coached witness falsely identify the subject in a police lineup. Finally, we have the subject taking a polygraph and regardless of the outcome inform the subject that the results confirms guilt. All such tactics are permissible provided such assertions are made verbally and the false statements are not made under oath in front of a judge and in the courtroom.

Invoking Guilt and Responsibility As previously discussed, guilt often leads to defensiveness, anxiety, and shame, a belief by some that they abandoned society's values. Or, still in others, guilt may result in a desire for retaliation—blaming others for their actions. Still in others, a guilt-ridden suspect may feel powerless and stymied in the ability to adequately respond to the situation, leading some to deliberately lie about their participation in the act under investigation to avoid facing the consequences. The reality is, however, few confessions are inspired solely by remorse and guilt (Educing Information 2006).

Manipulative Role-Playing Police are taught that an effective psychologically oriented interrogation often demands the ability to feign different personality traits or to act in a variety of roles. This may include projecting sympathy, understanding, and compassion while shielding one's personal judgments about the subject. The most well known among such strategies is the good cop/bad cop technique, which may be played with either one or two investigators or interrogators (Rafaeli 1991).

Implied False Promises and Incentives   Although promises of leniency have been ruled presumptively coercive since 1897 under the ruling *Bram versus United States* (1897), the courts continue to permit vague and indefinite promises. Specificity seems to be a key factor. For example, in one case, the suspect was repeatedly told that he had mental problems and needed psychological help rather than punishment and would get it provided that he confess. Although this approach by the interrogator implied leniency, the court upheld the conviction based on the confession (*Miller versus Fenton* 1986). The courts also permit interrogators or investigators to tell subjects that they will inform the court of the subject's cooperation, that showing of remorse will be a mitigating factor, or that they will help out every way they can if the subject confesses. Such assurances, while deceptive, are legal (Skolnick and Leo 1992).

The use of incentives, disincentives, and inducements—money, favors, gifts, special privileges (or their removal)—is commonly used within the intelligence community. However, in the law enforcement community, plea agreements are often used and may encourage testimony from those seeking lighter sentences.

These classic legacy techniques are still commonly taught and practiced despite the fact that far more creative, far less confrontational, and equally effective approaches are now available.

Multifaceted Social Influence and Persuasion Techniques

Newer techniques offer fresh, creative ways to influence cooperation from suspects or detainees, possess empirical research behind them—something largely lacking in former classic legacy interrogation techniques—and offer a noncoercive approach to gather reliable and useful information whether in a criminal or an intelligence context.

Largely rapport-based influence techniques, these multifaceted approaches come to us from experts who study the art and science behind persuasion, influence, and overcoming resistance from such fields as advertising, communications, negotiations, medicine, and behavioral science or psychology. By selectively choosing from among the menu of options laid out in this primer and tailored to a subject, law enforcement and intelligence interrogators may expand their options beyond those limited to classic legacy interrogation tactics—which can lead to greater opportunities for success.

First among Many: The Direct Approach   Whether in law enforcement or intelligence, all interrogations should routinely begin with this approach—it is a direct, unambiguous questioning of the subject (see the following figure).

The *direct approach* permits the interrogator to lessen the intensity so common in former interrogation models, and relies more on elicitation skills.

> ### Statistical Benefits of the Direct Approach
>
> Statistics from interrogation operations in World War II show that the direct approach was effective 90% of the time. In Vietnam and other operations, such as Grenada in 1983, Panama in 1989, and the first Gulf Wars in Kuwait and Iraq in 1991, the direct approach was 95% effective.
>
> The effectiveness of the direct approach in the early operations in Afghanistan, 2001 to 2002, and in Iraq in 2003 is still under study. However, unofficial statistics indicate that in these operations, the direct approach has been dramatically less successful.
>
> From *Army Field Manual 2–22.3, Human Intelligence Collector Operations*, Washington, DC, 2006.

For some suspects or detainees, the direct approach capitalizes on the *shock of capture phenomenon*—a brief psychological window of opportunity to exploit the confusion, the uncertainty, and the negative expectations going through the subject's mind immediately after arrest or capture. Despair typically sets in, as do feelings of confusion and fright. Consequently, the straightforward direct approach comes as a welcome relief to the subject. So plan to use this technique as long as the subject is answering the questions in a non-evasive, useful, and reliable manner.

Remember, too, that it is psychologically easier for a subject to tell the truth to someone who demonstrates an interest in him or her as a person, and who is seeking to understand why the subject committed the crime or act. While doing so, however, also keep in mind the need to avoid any emotional attachments to the subject through *transference* (see the following figure).

Use the direct approach as long as you believe the subject is answering your questions truthfully. Once the subject refuses to answer, falsely answers questions, or recants previous statements, your next move is to turn to more convincingly persuasive influence and counterresistance techniques.

Understanding Resistance and Persuasion   Resistance and persuasion represent the "yin and yang" of human interaction. Within interrogation tradecraft, an understanding of both is fundamental to achieving successful outcomes, especially when dealing with uncooperative subjects. So how may we promote change in a subject and gain his or her cooperation? For our purposes, there are two ways to do it. One way is to increase the motivation to cooperate and this is commonly represented by persuasive messaging. The second way to promote change is to decrease resistance through a number of alternative approaches. As emphasized by Knowles and Linn (2004) in their book *Resistance and Persuasion*, we may succeed in either of these approaches by generally increasing the positive forces for persuasion or by decreasing resistance by techniques that permit the receipt of the persuasive messages and convinces the subject to cooperate.

The Influence of Persuasive Messaging   Among the persuasive influence approaches, the most successful approaches focus their time and energy on attempts to win over an uncooperative subject rather than on negative interactions which are common in classic legacy tactics. These successful, persuasive, rapport-based approaches involve making the offer to cooperate more socially attractive through reasoning, trust, and credibility. Some of these approaches have been touched on in Chapter 4 but are worth repeating here to emphasize their selective value as part of an integrated interrogation strategy in the custodial phase of the interrogation.

Repetition and Message Relevance   A factor to weigh in any persuasive messaging is its degree of high or low personal relevance to the target recipient. The higher the personal relevance, the more effective the delivery and the attitudinal change. So in attempting to move an uncooperative suspect or detainee to a cooperative state, make sure that the message is relevant to him or her and their unique situation. And, of course, relevant arguments repeatedly heard are more persuasive than arguments heard only once. Just think of the repetitive advertising we are bombarded with every single day on the radio, television, and the Internet. It is the same idea.

Respect, Credibility, Trust, and Similarity   Respect and credibility weigh heavily on changing attitudes. The higher the credibility, respect, and trust the subject has in the persona of the interrogator, the more likely the desired interrogation outcomes will be achieved. As discussed in Chapter 3 of this primer, other characteristics that influence persuasion are forces of similarity and qualities aligned with rapport-building.

Consistency and Commitment   Commitment and consistency are powerful glues influencing the subject to a course of action. Inconsistency in your messaging threatens cooperation and compliance. So make sure you are consistent with your prior actions, statements, and requests. Getting people to commit to an action or a request is easier if the statements are compatible with prior requests. The greater the similarity of the content between the recent requests and the previous requests, the more persuasive is the foot-in-the-door effect.

Strong Positive Messaging   Rely on positive messaging to influence the subject's cooperation and set the stage for greater receptivity by the subject. Typically, too, rely on facts and strong arguments. The implication is that strong arguments are more effective than weak arguments. Accordingly, weak arguments are not merely unpersuasive but can actually be antipersuasive. In other words, weak messaging may sometimes move the recipient further away from the desired message position. So remember, in your contact with a suspect or detainee, formulate strong messages that suggest or imply positive consequences for the recipient.

Predicting the Future   Forcibly asking an uncooperative suspect or detainee to do something is generally ineffective in gaining compliance. This ineffectiveness is in large part due to the natural resistance most people experience when someone is asserting their will over them in a controlled setting. A better alternative may be simply to ask the subject "to predict what they would do if someone were to ask them to do XYZ and to weigh its advantages down the road." By focusing the subject on the future and the short- and long-term consequences of their decisions, an interrogator can help erode resistance in context to present circumstances. Predicting the future and imagining hypothetical future events focuses the subject away from the immediate unattractiveness of their present situation. It forces them to think about future implications where compliance seems more reasonable and easier to accept. Those interrogators who are savvy with these effects will find that making subtle suggestions to the subject to reflect on the future and to think more deeply about down-the-road consequences may help influence constructive choices in the present.

Appealing Narratives   In or out of the interrogation room, experienced leaders know the powerful influence narratives or stories have on people. When people are willing and able to listen to a message, strong arguments are more persuasive. And narratives are more persuasive when they appeal to the listener and when phrased in ways that allow easy understanding. Some qualities inherent in effective narratives are their wide audience appeal, vivid storylines, and use of humor. Such qualities are commonly found in parables, novels, songs, fantasy comics, television dramas and documentaries, and big-screen movies.

While the stories or narratives might be about external or inconsequential people and events (e.g., "I once knew someone who . . ."), the content and resolution of each story should mirror the subject's situation and identify a path out of a predicament. Because the story is ostensibly not about the subject, it does not engage resistance that would be sparked by an explicit rhetorical discussion about the subject's dilemma. Some researchers suggest that the use of narratives, in fact, may be one of the only strategies available for influencing the beliefs of those who are solidly predisposed to oppose outreach efforts and the most resistant to change—recalcitrant terrorist and true believers, for instance.

Influence by Self-Affirmation   Research shows that when selectively used, assisting the subject with self-affirmation—validating someone's self-worth or stroking someone's ego—may help to undermine resistance and leave individuals more open to persuasion. Provided that it is done with tact and discretion, this subtle form of manipulation could be used to get someone to do something he or she would not otherwise do. Or it could be used to get someone to divulge information.

To successfully use self-affirmation, you need to remember two important rules. First, the self-affirmation must be positive. Second, the self-affirmation must be somewhat compatible with your persuasive message, although not-in-your-face obvious. Whether or not self-affirmation creates a greater vulnerability to persuasion depends on the relationship between the topic of the self-affirmation and the gist of the persuasive message. If the topic of the self-affirmation is incompatible with the persuasive message, then self-affirmation may not lead to greater persuasion. Rather, they would result in resistance. For instance, you cannot say on the one hand, "I respect you for your honesty and integrity," and then turn around and say, "Now will you tell me a secret about your organization." You have to be a bit more sophisticated than that. Of course, in some cultures this idea of stroking someone's ego may yield a different outcome than in Western societies.

Norm of Reciprocity   Reciprocity possesses a powerful influence over people. This strategy involves the interrogator doing a small favor or providing the subject a gift before making a request to that person. In turn, the small favor creates a relationship that, in turn, engages a norm of reciprocity, an obligation to return the favor. As previously discussed, quite often, the only reciprocal favor a suspect or a detainee possesses is the information in his or her possession.

Influence of Intersecting Goals   Closely related to the norm of reciprocity is the ability to influence through intersecting goals. If it is carefully orchestrated by the interrogator, the subject comes to recognize—through implicit or explicit language—that the subject's actions can achieve some of his personal goals, such as release or better treatment. In an interrogation, the line between the subject's goal (e.g., early release or favorable treatment) runs directly through the interrogator's objective (i.e., gaining actionable intelligence, reliable evidence, or a confession).

Principle of Social Proof   Previously touched upon in Chapter 4, this persuasive strategy relies on the fact that most people follow the crowd and often use other people's actions as reference for what is appropriate and desirable. Thus, one strategy is for the interrogator to let the subject know that the choice offered to him or her to cooperate is the same one that others have accepted. Of course, the strategy can backfire on the interrogator, with some subjects offering counterarguments against cooperating. So the best approach is to use such an approach with caution.

Managing Anticipated Regret   Whenever an interrogator is trying to persuade a subject, one technique is to offer the subject a choice between two options—Alternative A and Alternative B—and lean the messaging in the direction of the preferred choice. As part of this messaging technique, the interrogator may ask the subject to anticipate the future regret that he or she might feel for selecting the less preferred option. "Before making your decision, just think a moment how you might feel in three years for not selecting Alternative A?" So remember the power of anticipated regret as an effective persuasion technique to help overcome resistance.

Capitalizing on Scarcity   Again, scarcity possesses a powerful motivating influence over people and was one of the primary principles of influence identified by Cialdini in his seminal 1984 book *Influence: The Psychology of Persuasion* and touched on in Chapter 4. He proposed that objects and opportunities appear more valuable when they are less available, even if those objects and opportunities have little intrinsic value. "If it is scarce, it must be valuable." Cialdini also offered a second interpretation of the power of scarcity that is much closer to our focus on interrogations and the previously discussed topic of anticipated regret. He suggests that as things become less and less available, subjects may perceive the loss of not getting them. "If you don't get it now, this offer might not come around a second time and you may regret not having it." Again, in this case, scarcity works by weakening the forces of resistance through the anticipation of future regret.

Avoid Attacks on Someone's Traditional Beliefs   Avoid threatening a person's deep-seated beliefs, such as a religion or culture. Negative messages, which vilify such beliefs, are not successful persuasion strategies. Long-standing attitudinal views in the subject—especially those steeped in history—tend to be particularly resistant to change. Expect a near insurmountable challenge if trying to convince someone otherwise. Your time and energy may be better spent avoiding such an approach and relying on the power of the persuasive social influence techniques we just discussed in this section.

Dealing with Resistance   What do we mean by the term *resistance*? It is basically refusing to make a change whether in behavior (refusing to answer questions truthfully) or in thinking (refusing to accept new viewpoints) in response to a request from the interrogator; and we know people resist or oppose persuasive attempts for a variety of reasons. Typically, it is a by-product of a preexisting belief, which the person insists on keeping (Intelligence Interviewing 2009). And like truthfulness and deceit, there are plenty of shades of gray in the degrees of resistance a subject may employ.

While suicide, physical outbursts, and debilitating hunger strikes represent the most extreme forms of resistance an interrogator may face, the following figure tries to capture other common resistance techniques you may encounter with a suspect or detainee.

Resistance Tactics Practiced by Uncooperative Subjects	
• Denying knowledge	• Claiming memory lapses
• Feigning illness	• Injecting lies within statements
• Recanting previous statements	• Claiming innocence
• Pacing selective release of information	• Shifting blame or knowledge to others
• Keeping completely silent	• Showing contempt
• Omitting statements deliberately	

What reinforces resistance in people? Basically, it is threat driven. When a person senses a threat from someone, resistance typically follows. Inside the interrogation room, this is reflected by the subject's unwillingness to cooperate. The greater the nature of the perceived threat—arbitrary, blatant, direct, and demanding—the greater the likelihood a detainee may resist. Without the threat, there is no resistance. Among the many other reasons not to cooperate could be distrust of the interrogator and weakness in argumentation of the persuasive message. Still, other reasons, according to Knowles and Linn (2004), may include the desire to avoid the punitive consequences of a previous act, conflicting biases, a cultural aversion to the change attempt, or any number of others.

In terms of the interrogation cycle, most conventional approaches to interrogation assume that once resistance surfaces, our options are limited; we either give up or ratchet up the pressure through increasingly confrontational coercive techniques. However, that is now up to challenge.

The moment resistance first happens might be a good starting point to shift strategies from a focus on persuasion tactics to acknowledging the resistance followed by reliance on techniques and tactics designed to defuse it. These alternative approaches work by decreasing the motivation, reasons, or incentives not to engage in resistant or uncooperative behavior (Knowles and Linn 2004).

Sidestepping Resistance   Successful interrogators focus their finite resources (e.g., time and energy) on subjects that present the most attractive risk-to-gain ratio. One way to do that is simply to ignore or avoid the need for the subject to revert to resistance in the first place. For an interrogator, you might sidestep resistance a number of ways. One way is to refrain from direct in-your-face or tell-me-everything demands by beginning with small, indirect, and less-threatening requests. Another way is simply "going next door." Occasionally, the information needed from a recalcitrant subject is obtainable from a willing subject or co-conspirator located in an adjoining cell.

Minimizing Requests   Another way to sidestep resistance is to minimize the initial request. The idea behind minimizing requests is that an initial small request may receive relatively little resistance.

Addressing Resistance Directly   Another approach seeks to reduce resistance by directly addressing its causes. One way is by offering some guarantee that the most feared outcome will not occur. If a subject is worried about feeling trapped, an interrogator might advise the subject, "Anytime you need a break, just let me know."

Distracting Resistance   Psychologists know that resistance requires attention and energy on the part of the subject to be optimally effective. Here, a mild distraction, such as engaging music or videos, or television, might occupy the subject's attention, thereby limiting the capacity to counterargue or resist. These considerations assume that the distraction is sufficient to interfere with resistance, yet weak enough not to obscure the message. Distractions can boomerang, of course, and lead to no persuasion. If a distraction is too intense, then it may become the focus of attention and your message may fail to even register with the subject.

Using Resistance to Promote Change   One of the most intriguing approaches to getting past resistance is to acknowledge it and use it. In a manner of speaking, this is the use of reverse psychology by interrogators. Reverse psychology is telling people not to do what you really want them to do. Here, an interrogator might precede a persuasive message by saying something like "I know you're determined not to listen to anything I say, but ..." When this works, the subject resists the acknowledgment or suggestion of resistance. Reverse psychology is a dangerous strategy if used recklessly because the interrogator is advocating something against his or her own interests. The targets of the influence—the subject—may take the suggestion at face value and act in accordance with the stated wishes, thereby thwarting the interrogator's aims. To be effective, reverse psychology requires that the interrogator has a real certainty that the subject will, in fact, oppose the suggestion and do exactly the opposite of what is requested in the messaging.

The Double-Bind Alternative Choice   This approach uses resistance to promote attitudinal or behavioral change by offering the subject a choice between two alternatives—Alternative A and Alternative B. Offering the subject a choice between two alternatives that achieve the same aims regardless of which alternative is chosen allows the subject to exhaust his or her resistance while still achieving the interrogator's aims. In psychology, this tactic of the alternative choice is labeled *double-bind* and commonly used by parents on children who are resistant to bedtime. In this case, the parent asks, "Do you want to brush your teeth first or do you want to put on your pajamas first?" It is a *double-bind* in the sense that both alternatives lead to the same outcome, in this case, going to bed. In the case of an interrogation, the interrogator can ask, "Which do you want to discuss first, A or B?" The outcome will be the same, but the subject feels he or she had control over the outcome by choosing which topic to address first.

Redefining Relationships   In redefining the interaction between the interrogator and the subject, a savvy interrogator might transform the situation away from an interrogation to something more benign or collaborative. Transforming the role of the suspect or detainee into the role of teacher or consultant implies that the interrogator takes on the role of learner; or transforming the role of suspect or detainee into that of an expert implies that the interrogator takes on the role of novice. In either case, the roles can indirectly disable a target's resistance. Such role transformations have many implications particularly for those who are long-term detainees of the intelligence community. First, it implies that both the interrogator and the subject are now working coopera- tively on a mutual goal. For instance, the interrogator might ask the subject to instruct, educate, and mentor on the beliefs of the subject's former cohort unit. By implication, the subject now has less need to feel threatened and is being respected for his or her knowledge. Second, such role transformations imply a longer-term relationship with more opportunities for interaction than a tradi- tional interrogator/subject relationship. Third, a long-term relationship implies that there will be future opportunities to reciprocate that may result from this interaction.

An Alternative Option to Defeat Resistance: Fear Appeals   Fear appeals (messages) are powerful strategies that attempt to change attitudes by relying on the negative emotion of fright to gain cooperation from a resistant subject. As a future-oriented negative emotion, it is closely tied to anticipated regret, scarcity, and perception management (Stephenson and Witte 1997).

Initially developed to promote healthy lifestyle changes and choices among medical patients—such as the increased risk of melanoma without routine, daily use of skin creams with sun-block protection—fear appeals generally contain two parts: (1) a fear component and (2) a desired response.

Typically, the subject first evaluates the fear component, which is defined by the message's severity. If the message initiates perceptions of fear that reach a certain threshold, then the subject next evaluates the effectuality of the desired response and the consequences for noncompliance. It is the combination of the perceived fear component coupled with the ability of the subject to comply with the desired response and the weighing of the conse- quences for noncompliance that determine successful outcomes.

Traditional research believed that moderate fear appeals were most effec- tive; low fear appeals did not portray sufficient degrees of negative conse- quences to influence subjects; and high fear appeals may have frightened subjects too much and increased resistance and defensive avoidance.

More recent research has changed views about high fear appeals. Such research demonstrates that properly communicated, strong or high fear appeals that are coupled with realistic recommendations that are easily and effectively executed by the subject, and avoids the perceived negative con- sequences, result in the highest degree of positive motivational influence. Alternatively, strong fear appeals that are coupled with ineffectual recom- mendations (too difficult, too time consuming, unrealistic), possess the lowest degree of influence on the subject. In the latter instance, subjects commonly engage in denial (e.g., "I'm not going to do it; no one else I know has done it"); defensive avoidance (e.g., "I'm just not going to think about the consequences"); or message manipulation (e.g., "They are just trying to scare me" or "What's the use? I'm screwed whether I do it or not"). So, where high fear messaging is coupled with effectual recommendations that are reasonably executed by the subject is where researchers saw the greatest success with the desired behavior change, patient compliance, and cooperation (Stephenson and Witte 1997).

Corroborate Outcomes

Too many interrogators treat a suspect's "I did it" statement as if it is automatically self-validating—even if it fails to be supported by logic or the evidence. Why? Because it too often validates the interrogator's assumption of the suspect's guilt—a kind of confirmation bias. Rather, interrogators and investigators need to learn to fact-check and evaluate the outcomes of their interrogations in a postmortem review. While doing so, they should treat admissions or confessions as neutral hypotheses to be tested against the evidence.

This process of corroborating outcomes is nothing new to the intelligence community and is easily adoptable to law enforcement interrogations as well. In the process of corroborating an interrogation, the interrogator is making a logical judgment. Typically, valid confessions will be supported by the evidence, the quality of the subject's responses, previous insights, forensics and, if available, witness statements. In the process, a guilty subject's admission or confession may reveal insights known only by the true perpetrator, lead to new evidence, explain anomalies at the crime scene, and be supported by forensics. False ones will not (Drizin and Leo 2004).

Too often, missing from this equation, at least in a law enforcement setting, is the need to inject an evaluation by the interrogator of confidence levels in the judgment of interrogation outcomes and in terms of guilt or innocence. Ascribing confidence levels in terms of *high, moderate,* or *low confidence* will ultimately help prosecutors in the decision to bring a case to trial. With so much at stake in terms of law enforcement credibility and society's concerns over prosecuting an innocent person, this step in the interrogation cycle should also call on the supervisor of the interrogator to actively participate in the evaluation process. By serving in a third-party review of the audiovisual recording and participating in the final determination of confidence levels, police supervisors inject accountability into the overall step of corroborating outcomes.

Decision to Refer to a Prosecutor, Release, or Detain and Repeat Cycle

This step represents the final stage of the law enforcement interrogation cycle. At this point, it should be fairly obvious if the facts warrant: referring the case to a prosecutor; releasing the suspect for lack of evidence; or whether, such as in the case of a detainee held on terror charges, requesting the subject be held for further questioning in a repeat of the entire cycle. Once referred, the case is now in the hands of the prosecutor.

The Intelligence Interrogation Cycle

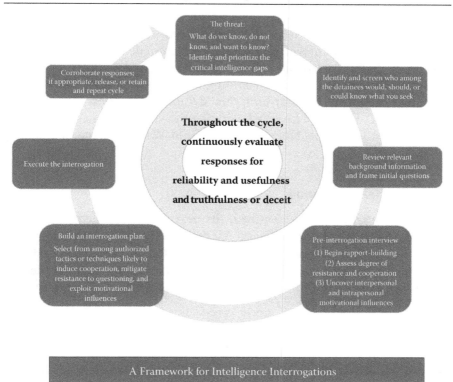

A Framework for Intelligence Interrogations

Similarities between the previous law enforcement interrogation cycle and this cycle for intelligence interrogations are apparent. In this case, however, we are talking about someone normally without U.S. Constitutional standing and interned outside of the United States so there is no need for the *Miranda* warning or waiver.

Identify Threats and Priority Intelligence Gaps

Starting at the top and working in a clockwise direction, notice that we begin the cycle with the threat and associated intelligence gaps—which are common to intelligence problem sets: What do we know about the threat? What do we not know relative to intelligence gaps? Which intelligence gaps are the most critical and time-sensitive and possess the highest priority to get filled first?

Screen Detainees

Next in sequential order, we need to screen and identify who among the detainee population might possess the information we seek. One suggested approach to identify an appropriate prisoner for interrogation or questioning is to make an initial determination of "who would know, could know, or should know" the information sought—a technique attributed to former U.S. Army master interrogator Tourison and practiced during his tours in Vietnam. For instance, a person claiming to be a local villager would know the names of those living near him, should know the location of the nearest medical clinic, and could know who among the villagers joined forces with local terrorist insurgents (Interrogation: World War II, Vietnam, and Iraq 2008).

Frame Initial Questions

Once a potential source is identified, the next step would be to review all relevant background information on the detainee; to refine your knowledge of the information gaps needed filling; and to start the process of framing initial questions in preparation for the pre-interrogation interview that, in most cases, may be the first face-to-face meeting between the interrogator and the detainee.

Perform Pre-Interrogation Interview

As with the noncustodial interrogation, one of the main goals of the pre-interrogation interview is to begin the initial efforts at rapport-building. Simultaneously, it also serves as an opportunity to evaluate the detainee's scope of knowledge, resistance posture, duplicity, willingness to cooperate in questioning, cognitive skills and intellect, and motivational influences. These factors may serve as valuable points of leverage if a formal interrogation is warranted.

Build and Execute Your Interrogation Strategy

Using all this relevant information as background, the interrogator next begins to develop an appropriate interrogation strategy tailored to the detainee. Such a plan requires the interrogator to select from among the authorized tactics and techniques likely to induce cooperation from the detainee, mitigate resistance, and help facilitate the greatest chances of success by persuasively influencing the detainee to provide useful and reliable answers to key questions.

The plan should also include identifying and issuing guidance to your team members; obtaining needed props, such as maps or photos, if needed; and rehearsing your questions in advance with your supporting linguist-interpreter; and consulting with any other interrogators who may have previously spoken with the detainee. Once completed, schedule the appropriate time and place for the interrogation and execute your strategy.

Corroborate Responses, Release, or Retain and Repeat Cycle

Once accomplished, the information received from the detainee must be vetted and corroborated. Once satisfied, the interrogation may terminate just as in the law enforcement cycle. In some cases, the detainee may be eligible for release. If, on the other hand, additional information is needed and the detainee appears to possess it, the interrogator may then repeat the cycle once again. Keep in mind, too, that throughout the intelligence interrogation cycle the detainee's responses are constantly evaluated for reliability and usefulness, truthfulness and deceit.

About Confessions

6

An interrogation is generally deemed successful in a law enforcement context when a suspect makes some sort of incriminating statement, voices an admission, or makes a full confession. Or, in an intelligence context, a detainee provides information needed to fill a critical information gap, provides time-critical or actionable intelligence about an imminent threat, or adds to our basic knowledge about the target group. So, too, is getting credible and reliable leads in either of these contexts.

What should a criminal interrogator expect in the way of confessions inside the interrogation room? In the United States, survey results over the past decade or more suggest that the rate of self-incriminating statements, admissions, or confessions range from 46% to 68% (Kassin, Leo, Meissner et al. 2007). British research shows a similar success pattern—in the range of approximately 50% to 55% of those interrogated (Educing Information 2006).

Three Major Factors Influencing Outcomes

From an interrogator's perspective, three factors influence confession outcomes. First is the strength of evidence believed to exist—real or imagined—by the suspect against himself or herself. Second is the amount of time spent by the interrogator inside the interrogation room with the suspect. Third is the number of tactics used on the suspect.

Strength of Evidence

The strength of the evidence—real or imagined—against a suspect is one of the best predictors of the likelihood of a confession. Additionally, suspects were significantly more likely to provide incriminating information during an interrogation in which strong evidence existed against them prior to questioning. In fact, the stronger these perceptions of evidence are, the more likely the suspect will confess, often resulting in some sort of admission in slightly more than 50% of cases. In cases where evidence was weak, confessions were rare—less than 10% of cases—and denials common—77% of cases (Educing Information 2006; Kassin, Leo, Meissner et al. 2007).

How do police, investigators, or interrogators create such perceptions? Possessing solid evidence helps—DNA or other forensics, security camera video, reliable witness statements, or victim testimony. But in the absence of tangible evidence or forensics, police sometimes bluff about the existence of evidence and make false claims such as "We've got your fingerprints." As previously discussed, the criminal courts do not forbid it. The only basic rules that seem to apply are that police cannot lie in front of a judge or in the courtroom and that they are prohibited from creating falsified tangible evidence. Apparently, the courts seem to draw a line between false verbal assertions made to the suspect and false tangible physical evidence manufactured to deceive the suspect, such as a hard copy forensic report. Inadvertently, such physical evidence could end up into the courtroom, so such acts are prohibited (Skolnick & Leo 1992).

Time

Longer interrogations commonly result in greater numbers of confessions over those that are far shorter. In 2004, the Federal Bureau of Investigation interrogation training literature claimed that "the chances of obtaining a confession increase 25 percent for every hour (up to 4 hours) of an interrogation" (Educing Information 2006). Experiences from law enforcement officers show that a custodial interrogation can vary in length from a few seconds—in cases when the suspect either immediately confesses or invokes *Miranda* rights and the interrogation is terminated—to about 5 hours for the longer ones. And, the 2007 survey of 631 law enforcement officers suggests that most criminal interrogation sessions are relatively brief with more than 90% of routine law enforcement interrogation sessions lasting about 1.50 hours. Yet the police survey did indicate that many suspects are often interrogated more than once over several days or weeks. The survey also demonstrated that the more serious the crime—murder or rape—the longer interrogators spend attempting to elicit incriminating information from a suspect (Kassin, Leo, Meissner et al. 2007). For the most part, time is a distinguishable difference in a military or intelligence setting where a knowledgeable terrorist or enemy combatant could be held for years and repetitively questioned—at least until interrogators are convinced that the detainee has exhausted his or her knowledge, no longer poses a threat, the conflict ends, or the need to intern the detainee no longer exists.

Number of Tactics

In general, the larger the number of tactics used inside the interrogation room, the more likely one of them will resonate with the subject and result in

a confession, an admission, or an incriminating statement. In a field observa-
tional study of nearly 200 interrogations, Leo (1996) observed the number of
tactics a detective employed per interrogation ranged from zero (e.g., the suspect spontaneously confessed or the detective did not genuinely try to elicit a
confession) to 15 for the longest one. However, the average was approximately
five. The higher numbers of tactics seemed dependent on three variables:
(1) seriousness of the crime—the more serious the crime, the higher the number of interrogation tactics used in a custodial setting; (2) race and ethnicity—
minorities were subjected to far more tactics over their white counterparts;
and (3) strength of evidence—the stronger the evidence, the fewer tactics used
since there was less need for incriminating evidence (Leo 1996).

As highlighted at the beginning of this chapter, statistically expect about
50% of the suspects to make some sort of incriminating statement to the
interrogator. Of that number, increasing concerns are being raised by judicial
watch groups over the validity of these success rates in light of recent empirical studies, demonstrating that false confessions do occur. False confessions
most notably occur when heavy-handed, manipulative, and deceptive techniques are employed by relentless and unethical interrogators.

> There is a common belief that people do not make unreliable or false state-
> ments unless they're tortured or mentally ill. And I would explain . . . that's
> not the case, sometimes people do make false statements, even if they're not
> physically tortured or mentally ill, that there . . . is psychological research
> that explains how certain [interrogation] techniques can lead people to make
> the decision to confess whether they're guilty or innocent. (*Vent versus State
> of Alaska* 2003)

Other Influential Variables

Age

Older suspects and detainees, generally those older than 26 years, seem to
cope better with the unfamiliarity and demands of police interrogation than
younger ones. A possible explanation may be that older suspects are often
better equipped psychologically to cope with the demands of an interrogation. Another possible explanation is that older suspects are more likely
to understand and assert their legal rights during an interrogation. There
is also case law that demonstrates that younger suspects are more likely to
confess than older suspects. One possible explanation for this phenomenon
is that younger people, especially juveniles, do not think through the long-
term implications of their confession and are commonly influenced by family members to come clean. In a survey of nearly 25,000 juveniles—with an

average age of 15.5 years—from seven European countries, 14% reported giving a false confession (Redlich, Summers & Hoover 2009). In other instances, the National Registry of Exonerations statistics suggest that young people in particular are more prone to admitting guilt for crimes they did not commit. Nearly 40% of exonerations for crimes allegedly committed by youths under 18 years old in the last quarter of the century involved false confessions compared with 11% for adults.

Gender

As of 2013, nearly 93% of persons arrested and imprisoned for serious crimes were male. Females, despite comprising slightly more than half of the U.S. population, make up about 7% of the prison population in the United States (DOJ 2014). In terms of violent crimes, such as homicides, males in 80% of the cases killed a stranger or a nonfamily member. Females, on the other hand, in about 60% of the cases killed their spouse, an intimate acquaintance, or a family member. It also seems that for their crimes, females generally receive lighter sentences by the courts. In general, men are nearly 16 times more likely to be incarcerated than women for a crime. In terms of confession rates, a comprehensive study conducted in Britain in a survey of 4250 arrests among 10 police stations in England and Wales concluded that females confess at higher rates than males, a 73% admission rate for females versus 52% for males (Phillips & Brown 1998).

Race and Ethnicity

For context and background for what we are about to discuss next, it is important to know that blacks (non-Hispanics) make up about 13.2% of the U.S. population; whites (non-Hispanics) about 62%; Hispanics about 17.4%; and Asians about 5%, according to U.S. Census statistics for 2014.

According to 2013 Department of Justice crime statistics, black men represented the largest proportion of sentenced male inmates at year-end at nearly 37%; white males made up about 32%. Meanwhile, Hispanic men made up 22% of the prison population. Among females, whites comprised 49% of the female prison population in 2013, while black females 22%.

In terms of incarceration rates for males, the statistics show that black men were two times more likely to be incarcerated than Hispanics and seven times more likely to receive prison sentences than white criminals. Among women, the imprisonment rates for black females, as a percentage to their population, is twice that of white females (DOJ 2014). Overall, the numbers show nearly 3% of the black male population in prison. Among the many factors to account for larger conviction rates among black males and females is an assessment that whites are getting better plea bargains than blacks (Bureau of Justice Assistance 2011).

Mental State and Psychological Factors

Research from self-reported surveys of previously incarcerated false confessors were significantly different on a number of measures relating to negative life events, particularly being bullied or expelled from school, substance abuse, self-harming behaviors, cognitive skill deficits, and mental health issues. Overall, the general picture that emerges is that false confessors have more mental health-related issues than those who do not make false confessions. Additionally, such survey results are consistent with mental illness as a recognized risk factor for false confessors (Redlich, Summers & Hoover 2009).

Previous Convictions

With regard to prior prison experience, the likelihood of a denial of guilt was twice as great in cases where the suspect had already been to prison. Such suspects who have had several previous convictions are more likely to know and assert their legal rights, more familiar with the probable consequences of making self-incriminating admissions and confessions, and more familiar with the police environment and interrogations. Consistent with expectations, suspects with previous felony records were four times more likely to invoke their *Miranda* rights than suspects without previous convictions and suspects with previous convictions were less likely to confess to the alleged offense than first-time offenders (Educing Information 2006).

Type of Offense

The more serious the offense and the greater the stakes in terms of perceived and real punishment, the less likely a suspect would confess. In general, suspects interrogated for property offenses confessed more often than suspects of violent offenses (Mitchell 1983; Neubauer 1974).

Access to Legal Advice

Contrary to expectations, access to an attorney does not appear to reduce the overall confession rate in major ways. In other words, even with a high proportion of suspects being provided legal advice, suspects still confessed in slightly more than half of all cases (Gudjonsson & Hilton 1998).

Miranda Rights

Even though invoking *Miranda* is a potentially powerful tool for suspects to avoid interrogation, multiple law enforcement surveys since 1996 demonstrate that roughly four out of five criminal suspects typically waive their rights and agree to enter questioning. In percentage terms, that is approximately an 80% waiver rate (Leo 1996).

Among the 574 U.S. police officers who participated in the 2007 self-reported survey of law enforcement officers, respondents estimated that about 68% of suspects fully waived their rights, while an additional 13% initially waived their rights but then reversed themselves and invoked them (Kassin, Leo, Meissner et al. 2007). This generally tracks with previous survey results that claim that about 20% of suspects choose to terminate questioning and invoke their *Miranda* rights from the start (Kassin, Leo, Meissner et al. 2007).

Other Considerations

As we have just discussed, many variables influence confessions. The following figure tries to summarize other factors that may impede a confession or lead some to deny knowing something important.

Factors Inhibiting Confessions
1. Fear of legal consequences—financial liberty, death
2. Professional reputational concerns—the higher the social standing, the greater reluctance to confess
3. Personal shame—desire to keep family and friends ignorant of activities
4. Fear of retaliation—against his or her person or family
5. Ideological or societal beliefs and commitments
6. Response to coercively unfair techniques or perceptions of ill-treatment
7. Initial success with lies, which reinforces further deception and denials

Wrongful Convictions

No one really knows the extent of the problem within the criminal justice system. Yet the reality that greater numbers of formerly convicted subjects are being exonerated by the courts, many of whom have served decades behind bars, suggests some sort of breakdown in our criminal justice system.

Prominent among the advocacy groups probing the causes of wrongful convictions and evaluating why so many innocent persons have served time in prison are the National Registry of Exonerations, a project of the University of Michigan Law School, and the Innocence Project at the Benjamin N. Cardozo School of Law at Yeshiva University. Founded in 2012, the National Registry provides detailed information about every known exoneration in the United States since 1989—cases in which a person was wrongly convicted of a crime and later cleared of all the charges based on new evidence that ascertain innocence. Predating the registry by 20 years, the Innocence Project was established in 1992 to help prove the innocence of convicts through DNA testing.

As of mid-March 2015, the National Registry database held over 1,564 exonerated persons, some of whom spent decades behind bars. As of mid-2015, the Innocence Project held over 325 former defendants exonerated by DNA testing, including 18 internees who were formerly on death row. In total, these 1,564 former internees spent nearly 14,000 years in prison—on average, about 9 years each. Almost all were imprisoned for years; 41% for 10 years or more; 62% for at least 5 years.

As demonstrated by the Innocence Project and the National Registry, wrongful convictions are far too common within the criminal justice system. Among the 1,564 internees previously discussed, nearly 46% were falsely convicted of homicide, nearly 30% were falsely convicted of sexual assault including child sex abuse, and nearly 15% falsely convicted for other violent crimes. Major contributing factors to their wrongful convictions included the following:

- False confessions: 13%
- Misleading or false evidence: 22%
- Eyewitness misidentification: 34%
- Official (police or prosecutorial) misconduct: 46%
- Perjury or false accusations: 55%

Among the most serious of violent crimes—homicides, sexual assaults, and child abuse cases—wrongful conviction statistics are even more dramatic according to the National Registry. In specific crime categories:

- Perjury or false accusations are highest in child sex abuse cases (81%) and homicide cases (67%).
- Official misconduct is highest in homicide cases (59%) and child sex abuse cases (46%).

- Mistaken eyewitness identifications are highest in robbery cases (83%) and adult sexual assault cases (72%).
- False or misleading evidence are highest in adult sexual assault cases (33%) and child sex abuse cases (23%).
- False confessions are highest in homicide cases (21%).

Interrogation-Induced False Confessions

Within the context of wrongful convictions, a false confession is an admission of an act the confessor did not commit. Research suggests that false confessions are powerfully persuasive and that many false confessions contain detailed narratives and accurate facts that appear to betray guilty knowledge (Kassin 2012).

The idea of false confessions is a foreign concept to most people. Many have difficulty comprehending the situational factors which would lead an innocent person to confess to an act they did not commit—particularly to an act which is criminal in nature and could result in a long incarceration in prison or even the death penalty. Yet false confessions show up in nearly 15% of all cases in the National Registry and nearly 30% of DNA exoneration cases according to the Innocence Project. In fact, false confessions are counterintuitive in part because these false statements come from the defendant themselves and, in part, because they often contain facts that were not publicly known. In some circumstances, false confessions may include statements of motive, even apologies and remorse. Such detailed admissions indicate that the innocent confessor may have obtained the information from either "leading" questions inside the interrogation room or other secondary sources of external influence (American Psychological Association 2014). The following figure captures the most vulnerable among the population to interrogation-induced false confessions and to external influences.

Demographics of Common False Confessors
1. Naively trusting juveniles
2. Cognitively and intellectually disabled
3. Persons with psychotic and personality disorders
4. Targets of excessively physical or psychologically coercive interrogators

As previously discussed, researchers recognize that interrogation-induced false confessions tend also to correlate with excessively lengthy interrogations. In support of such findings, Drizin and Leo (2004) documented 125 cases of proven false confessions in conjunction with the Northwestern University School of Law and its Center on Wrongful Convictions. Of those in the sample who went to trial attempting to reclaim their innocence, over 80% were wrongly convicted based on interrogation-induced confessions. In the study, the average length of the interrogation was 16.3 hours, far exceeding the norms of most police interrogations.

The major causes of interrogation-induced false confessions are the interrogator's use of psychologically relentless tactics and contamination error reflected through the following:

- Repetitive and suggestive questioning that exposes the subject to new information not previously discussed or known to the subject which is then adopted by the subject in future retelling of events.
- Deceptively telling the subject that others have already provided the details and, to escape the interrogation, all the subject needs to do is confirm what everyone already knows.
- The use of positive feedback, incentives, or encouragement when the information confirms or is consistent with the interrogator's perceived assumptions or biases.
- The use of negative feedback, disincentives, or discouragement when the information refutes or is inconsistent with the interrogator's perceived assumptions or biases.
- Coercively repeating a question, intimidating, badgering or browbeating the subject until the interrogator got the response sought.
- Telling the suspect or detainee that he or she may have had a memory lapse and then convincing the subject to accept the interrogator's version of events to fill the void.
- Retelling a distorted version of previously elicited testimony by the investigator or interrogator to confuse the subject and in an effort to have a false narrative adopted and recited by the subject in subsequent testimony.

In response to these manipulative interrogation tactics, Professor Richard Leo (2009) from the University of San Francisco's School of Law identifies three major types of interrogation-induced false confessions:

- Voluntary false confession: A false confession voluntarily and knowingly given in response to little or no police pressure and for a variety of reasons, including a pathological desire for notoriety, need for self-punishment, mental impairment, or a desire to protect the actual perpetrator.

- Compliant false confession: A confession knowingly given to put an end to a harsh interrogation. Many adults with mental disabilities, younger adolescents, and even normal adults who respond badly to stress often succumb to compliant false confessions. In other cases, an innocent person gives way to social pressure during interrogation, especially juveniles or children influenced by their parents. They are led to believe that the short-term benefits of a false confession outweigh the long-term costs of prolonged interrogation. A famous example of a compliant false confession took place in the 1989 Central Park Jogger Case, in which five young suspects were told that they could end their lengthy and coercive interrogations in connection with the rape and murder of a female victim if they provided statements placing themselves at the scene of the crime and incriminated each other.
- Persuaded false confession: A false confession knowingly given by an innocent suspect who comes to doubt the reliability of his or her memory and thus comes to believe that he or she may have committed the crime despite no actual memory of having done so. Also called *internalized false confession*, this type of confession is admittedly rare and yet persuasive when entered into evidence.

Regardless of the age, mental capacity, or a host of other extenuating factors, what all false confessors seem to have in common is the decision, at some point during the interrogation process, that confessing will be more beneficial to them than maintaining their innocence and enduring harsh treatment at the hands of an aggressive interrogator. And, as we now know, repeated and suggestive questioning at the hands of an aggressive interrogator may implant false memories, elicit false information, and coerce a vulnerable subject into giving false testimony.

In an ironic twist, the one case that catapulted John E. Reid and his methodology to national prominence in the 1950s speaks to these points directly. The case involved the murder of Nancy Parker and husband-defendant Darrel Parker, who was wrongly charged with her murder. It took nearly 40 years to overturn his conviction and 57 years to officially pronounce him innocent. The account is drawn from the National Registry of Exonerations with its permission. The registry's summary of the case was written by Senior Researcher Maurice Possley (2012).

In 1956 Darrel Parker, a forester in Lincoln, Nebraska, was convicted of murdering his wife solely by a confession—recanted almost immediately after—and given under coercive circumstances after 12 hours of intense interrogation by John E. Reid who served as his interrogator. At the end of his interrogation, Reid said Parker confessed. Parker recanted the confession almost immediately, but it was rejected. Parker went on trial in the Lancaster County Court of Common Pleas in May, 1956. The evidence against him consisted almost solely of his confession. He was convicted by a jury on June 2, 1956. Parker was sentenced to life in prison. After his initial appeal was denied, Parker filed a federal petition for a writ of habeas corpus. In February 1969, the U.S. Court of Appeals for the Eighth Circuit ruled that the confession had been coerced and ordered Parker retried or released. The state of Nebraska appealed and the U.S. Supreme Court reversed and sent the case back to the trial court for a hearing on whether the confession was voluntary. Parker was released on his own recognizance in December 1969. After the Supreme Court ruling, Parker agreed to waive the hearing, the confession was found to be voluntary, and his conviction was reinstated. Days later, the Nebraska Board of Pardons commuted his sentence to 25 from 45 years in prison. Parker was then paroled. He moved to Illinois.

Five years later, in 1975, Wesley Peery was convicted of murdering a woman in Havelock, Nebraska, and was sentenced to death. While on death row, he told his lawyers about 13 other murders he had committed—but refused to allow his attorney to tell anyone about them until after he died. One of those murders was Nancy Parker. Peery had a meticulous memory of the murder and provided a multitude of details that coincided with the evidence in the crime. After Peery died in 1988, his confession to killing Nancy Parker was revealed. Based on Peery's confession, Parker sought a pardon. In 1991, he was granted a full pardon by the Nebraska Board of Pardons. In 2011, attorneys for Parker filed a claim for $500,000 under the Nebraska Wrongful Conviction and Imprisonment Act. In August 2012, the state of Nebraska issued a declaration of innocence to Parker and agreed to pay him $500,000. Attorney General Jon Bruning publicly declared that Parker was wrongly convicted based on a false confession and official misconduct and apologized on behalf of the State of Nebraska.

Eyewitness Misidentification

Eyewitness misidentification is one of the major causes of wrongful conviction nationwide, playing a role in nearly 35% of convictions that were subsequently exonerated. As far back as the late 1800s, experts knew that eyewitness identification is all too susceptible to error. In 1932, Yale law professor Edwin Borchard formally identified eyewitness error as an important factor that contributed to the erroneous conviction of innocent people. Now, more than 80 years later, his findings are repeatedly echoed in many of the wrongful convictions in the National Registry of Exonerations. Despite the fact that empirical research has demonstrated for decades that witnesses can be rather unreliable, there is still much to learn. According to the Innocence Project, witness memory is like any other evidence at a crime scene. It must be carefully preserved and retrieved methodically.

Scientific research demonstrates that when it comes to eyewitness testimony there is no relationship between confidence and accuracy. This is particularly true of highly emotionally charged events in our lives; and certainly seeing a violent crime as a witness fits into that category. To help illustrate this point, here is an abbreviated snapshot of events surrounding the 2014 killing of Michael Brown in Ferguson, Missouri. The accounts below emphasize the vulnerability of eyewitness testimony to contamination error and memory distortion.

> On August 9, 2014, black teenager Michael Brown was shot and killed by white police officer Darren Wilson in Ferguson, Missouri. Wilson tried to stop the teenager in the middle of a street for a possible theft of some cigarillos from a convenience store. Upon confronting Brown, Wilson claimed the teen, who was 18 years old, attacked him and struggled to grab his police pistol. A companion of Brown claimed that, to the contrary, the teenager was compliant to the police officer's demands and had his hands in the air and screamed, "Don't shoot!" The incident ignited months of violent rioting and racial tensions by hundreds, perhaps thousands, of Missourians and other out-of-state civil rights advocates who took to the streets chanting, "Hands up, don't shoot!" Many residents claimed Brown's civil rights were violated. For context, Ferguson is a city of 21,000 residents, two-thirds black, yet its police force had only three black officers. Many young black men in the city felt targeted by the police and resented it.
>
> A grand jury convened. The U.S. Attorney General personally provided oversight in the case along with an army of FBI investigators who sought out witnesses and their testimony. Over 60 eyewitnesses came forward claiming first-hand, yet conflicting, memories of what happened on the day of the shooting. On cross-examination, many changed their stories under questioning; others could not be believed at all, including one woman who claimed she might have dreamed about seeing the confrontation between the officer and Brown. Some admitted lying. Other versions were largely inconsistent with forensic evidence. And in some cases, witnesses admitted they were afraid to come forward because they feared reprisals from the enraged community if their stories supported Wilson's account of the events. In the end, the testimony of about 6 eyewitnesses was accepted as credible by the grand jury over the testimony of over 50 others. Officer Darren Wilson was exonerated of any guilt in November 2014 and the mantra "Hands up, don't shoot!" false. Months later, in March 2015, a federal civil rights investigation of Wilson did the same.

Jailhouse Informants

According to the Innocence Project, jailhouse informants are responsible for nearly 20% of wrongful conviction cases overturned through DNA testing. Such statistics and exonerations show that informants commonly lie and their testimony often unreliable. Why? Because falsely testifying in exchange of an incentive—typically a sentence reduction—is often the last resort of a desperate inmate. For someone not yet in prison, providing false testimony may be a desperate move to avoid going to jail (Innocence Project 2015).

Too often, law enforcement officials who seek out informants share extensive background information on cases—inadvertently feeding informants with what they need in the way of information to provide the false testimony. In other cases, statements from people with incentives to testify—particularly incentives that are not disclosed to the jury—serve as core evidence in convicting an innocent person. Unfortunately, incentivized informants continue to testify in courtrooms around the country today. Why? In cases without any forensic DNA evidence, the incentivized testimony from informants is often the only evidence a prosecutor has of a suspect's guilt (Innocence Project 2015).

Owning Up to the Problem

Recent research suggests that confessions, eyewitnesses, and informants—especially in the absence of other evidence—are persuasively convincing among police, prosecutors, and juries. For investigators, gaining a confession from a criminal suspect often results in overlooking other exculpatory evidence or leads—even in cases in which the confession is internally inconsistent and contradicted by external evidence or a by-product of an excessively long and coercive interrogation. When such false confessions or false testimony is injected into the judicial system, the results can be severe and dramatic for all sides in the criminal justice system:

- Frequently resulting in innocent persons going to prison.
- Corrupting other evidence from lay witnesses and forensic experts—producing an illusion of false support for a conviction.
- Undermining public confidence in law enforcement and the justice system.
- Causing long-term resentment by subjects coerced into false confessions and found guilty.
- Serving as a challenge for police, judges, and juries who cannot easily distinguish between uncorroborated true and false confessions.

Moreover, recognizing that we got it wrong after the fact is a tragic lesson, especially as evidenced by the large numbers of innocent defendants whose convictions are overturned thanks to modern DNA testing and other improvements in forensics. These lessons should force us to review the interrogation process and ask ourselves what we might do differently to help mitigate wrongful convictions.

Minimizing False Confessions

Here are some suggestions that find broad consensus among our nation's law enforcement and criminal justice experts.

Electronically Record Interrogations
False confessions could be greatly reduced if the police were required to electronically record the entirety of all custodial interrogations of suspects. Videotapes create the opportunity for various criminal justice officials to more closely monitor both the quality of police interrogation and the reliability of confession statements. Unlike some potential reforms, the recording of police interrogations favors neither the defense nor the prosecution, but only the pursuit of reliable and accurate fact-finding. In fact, the 2007 survey among the 631 law enforcement officers revealed that 81% of the respondents favored recording interrogations from start to finish (Kassin, Leo, Meissner et al. 2007).

Educate in False Confessions
According to Drizin and Leo (2004), police investigators and interrogators—and for that matter intelligence officers too—need better training in the psychology of interrogations, decision-making by suspects, and confessions. In support of such aims, experts suggest these four areas for continued emphasis in professional education programs for interrogators and police investigators:

1. **Impact of select legacy tactics on innocent suspects:** Interrogators need to be taught that psychologically manipulative legacy interrogation techniques can and do cause innocent suspects (who are cognitively normal) to falsely confess. More importantly, interrogators need to be shown why such interrogation methods may lead to the decision to confess from the guilty as well as the innocent.
2. **The need to corroborate confessions:** Police interrogators need to be trained better to recognize their own biases, to initially treat an admission or confession as a neutral hypothesis to be tested against objective case facts, and to systematically validate their confidence levels of a suspect's postadmission narrative or confession. Additionally, detectives need to be taught that the proper way to assess the reliability of a suspect's confession is by analyzing the fit of the suspect's postadmission narrative or confession against the

underlying crime facts to determine whether it reveals guilty knowledge and whether it is corroborated by existing evidence. Assuming that there is no contamination, a guilty suspect's postadmission narrative will reveal knowledge known only to the true perpetrator, the police, or both; lead to new or derivative evidence; explain seeming anomalies or otherwise inexplicable crime facts; and are able to be corroborated by existing physical and medical evidence. An innocent suspect's postadmission narrative will typically reveal just the opposite.

3. **Understanding special category persons:** Interrogators need to receive specialized training in how to interrogate persons with developmental disabilities and young juveniles, two subgroups of suspects who appear to be particularly vulnerable to falsely confessions or making false statements. Because juvenile suspects share many of the same characteristics as the developmentally disabled—notably their eagerness to comply with adult authority figures, impulsivity, immature judgment, and inability to recognize and weigh risks in decision-making—they are at risk of falsely confessing when exposed to manipulative, psychological interrogation techniques.

4. **Limiting reliance on nonverbal body language:** Police interrogators need to be retrained to understand that they are not human lie detectors, and that they endanger the innocent when they guess the meanings behind the many hundreds of possible combinations of eye, hand, and body movements. Yet based on legacy interrogation methodologies and instruction, that is exactly what our nation's police interrogators have come to rely on—a psychology of human lie detection that is empirically proven to be unreliable and flawed. Such judgments are highly prone to error and have misled interrogators and investigators to believe in their inordinate abilities to discern truth from lies. Rather, quite typically the opposite is true. Remember, confidence in someone's abilities at lie detecting does not necessarily lead to greater accuracy.

Eyewitness Reforms

Additionally, the Innocence Project suggests a range of reforms to improve eyewitness identification accuracy, particularly for live person and photo lineups. These reforms have received endorsement by the National Institute of Justice, the American Bar Association, and the National Academy of Sciences. The benefits of these reforms are corroborated by over 30 years of peer-reviewed comprehensive research (Innocence Project 2015).

Double-Blind Procedure/Blind Administrator

A *double-blind* lineup is one in which neither the administrator nor the eye-witness knows for certain whether the likely suspect will be present among those in the live person or photo lineup. This prevents the administrator of the lineup from providing inadvertent or intentional verbal or nonverbal cues that may influence the eyewitness' selection and prevents the administrator from affirming the accuracy of any selection.

Sequential Presentation of Lineups

When combined with a "blind" administrator, presenting lineup members one by one (sequentially), rather than all at once (simultaneously), has been proven to significantly increase the overall accuracy of eyewitness identifications.

"I Don't Know" Instructions

Instructions are a series of statements issued by the lineup administrator to the eyewitness that deter the eyewitness from feeling compelled to make a selection. They also prevent the eyewitness from looking to the lineup administrator for feedback during the identification procedure. One of the recommended instructions includes the directive that the suspect may or may not be present in the lineup.

Composing the Lineup

The photographs or the persons in the live lineup should be selected to avoid bringing unreasonable attention to the suspect. Nonsuspect photographs and/or live lineup members (fillers) should be selected based on their resemblance to the description provided by the eyewitness—as opposed to their resemblance to the most likely police suspect.

Postselection Confidence Statements

Immediately following the lineup procedure, the eyewitness should provide a statement, in his or her own words, that expresses the level of confidence he or she has in the identification made. This could be as simple as stating high, medium, or low confidence.

Recording or Documenting Lineups

Ideally, the lineup procedure should be electronically recorded. If this is impracticable, an audio or written record should be made. Such recordings will help to demonstrate the existence or absence of external influences on the witness and affirm the fairness of the lineup process.

Unmasking Deception

7

A lie is an intentional act to conceal, fabricate, or distort information with the aim of creating a belief in another person's mind that the deceiver knows is untrue. For an interrogator, uncovering deception and lies can be of high-stake relevance with serious consequences for both the interrogator and the deceiver. At stake could be the public's safety, the lives of our military and police officers, and even the security of our nation. For the deceiver, it could mean the difference between going free or spending many years in a prison or a POW-holding facility. In lying and deceiving, a suspect or detainee may do the following:

- Provide false descriptions of events, persons, or things to mislead.
- Offer false denials to shield knowledgeability, culpability, and guilt.
- Manipulate or omit facts (called *half-truths*) to confuse the investigator.
- Hedge or equivocate to shield true thoughts, beliefs, feelings, and knowledge.

Why do deceivers typically lie? For most crime suspects or detainees, the common motivations for deceit are these four major factors:

1. Fear: Avoiding retaliation or legal sanctions, such as financial penalties, loss of liberty, or even death; the greater the penalty, the greater the motivation to deceive.
2. Shame: Reputational concerns and social standing; the higher the social standing, the greater the reluctance to confess.
3. Desire to get something: Tangible or intangible, personal or for a group.
4. Desire to protect someone or something: On a personal or group level.

Intelligence and law enforcement professionals know that all inconsistencies in the source's words do not necessarily indicate a lie, just as consistency is not necessarily a guarantee of the truth. For instance, a falsehood based on self-delusion or a mistaken belief does not qualify as a deceptive lie. Know, too, that interrogators who are overtly biased in their beliefs or assumptions as they enter the interrogation room make themselves vulnerable to deception and manipulation by a perceptive suspect or detainee who is quick thinking enough to respond to questions in anticipation of the interrogator's expectations.

Offset the Liar's Advantage

Detecting deception is not easy, and it is compounded by the fact that deceiver may have a clear advantage over the investigator or interrogator who is engaged in trying to unravel truths from lies. In fact, practiced liars have a very good chance of succeeding in their deception and not getting caught. Recent research in deception at the Northwestern University suggests that the more frequently a person lies, the better a person gets at it. In short, rehearsals and practice seem to help (Hu, Chen & Fu 2012). Additionally, successful deception serves as its own form of reinforcement and, for some, a thrill that further increases chances of even more lies. The research also suggests that the faster a person's ability to lie, the more difficult it is to detect the lie—evidently, the ability to think fast on your feet helps (Anyaso 2012).

To help offset this advantage, researchers suggest that investigators and interrogators inject unanticipated *filler* questions into their interrogation strategy that liars might not anticipate (Vrij, Granhag, Mann et al. 2011). Such filler questions should be designed to require repeated honest responses that are common knowledge to both the respondent and the questioner. The technique is based on the premise that increasing the predominance of honest responses to filler questions makes competing deceptive responses—lying— more difficult when substantive investigative questions are asked. The higher the number of irrelevant filler questions that require honest responses, the more difficult it is to reverse course when asked relevant investigative questions (Hu, Chen & Fu 2012).

Integrity Is Not a Stable Trait

Trustworthiness and deception are not pure black-and-white issues. There are plenty of shades of gray or gradations between the two. Consequently, you should expect that most narratives or storylines from subjects will contain intentional half-lies and half-truths; others are unintentional, perhaps attributable to flawed memories.

Honesty and deception are also situation dependent. In other words, someone who has been honest in the past will not necessarily be honest in the future, and vice versa. Along these lines of thought, Northeastern University professor and psychologist David DeSteno (2014a) suggests that many people who identify themselves as morally upstanding will act dishonestly to benefit themselves if they believe that they will not get caught. So remember that a reputation for trustworthiness earned under one set of circumstances cannot be relied on to hold up when circumstances, trade-offs, and accountability change.

To understand why, we need to abandon the notion that most people wrestle with good and evil impulses, which serves as a fundamental theory for many of the traditional legacy interrogation methodologies. Rather, focus on the two types of gains: short-term and long-term for the topic under discussion. It is the situational trade-off and the degree of risk versus gain that a person is willing to take when deciding to lie and deceive or tell the truth (DeSteno 2014a).

Such insights raise important red flags. If everyone is capable of lies, a good question for an investigator or interrogator to ask himself or herself during a debriefing, interrogation, or custodial interview is this: "Is this criminal suspect, detainee, or captured spy lying about something we care about at this given moment and on this critical topic of interest?"

People Make Poor Lie Detectors

People are generally not very good at spotting liars via behavioral cues. A number of studies, over many decades, have demonstrated that individuals perform no better than chance at detecting deception and that detection training tends to produce only small and inconsistent increments of improvement in performance. Empirical research by Bond and DePaulo (2006) demonstrate that people exhibit on average an overall 54% accuracy rate (47% for lies; 61% for truths) under the best of circumstances. Such findings challenge the uncorroborated claims that training in the detection of complex nonverbal indicators or cues, common in legacy interrogation manuals, can increase accuracy rates to 80% to 85% or better. In fact, any improvements have been typically very small. In one of the more successful studies, the untrained control group achieved a baseline success rate of 53.4% with detecting lies and truths, while the trained observers attained a success rate of 57.66%. Other studies demonstrated far worse results (Kassin & Fong 1999).

Trained experts, such as the police, perform only slightly better than ordinary people, if at all. Law enforcement professionals, like all people, are apparently no better at discriminating between truth and deception in others even with training (Kassin, Leo, Meissner et al. 2007).

Yet law enforcement officers consistently rate themselves above average when it comes to assessing their abilities to detect deception and lies. This confidence in their abilities does not translate into greater accuracy than that of the average person at distinguishing between truth-tellers and liars according to a number of respected research studies. For example, when participants in a 2007 survey of 631 law enforcement officers were asked to rate their own deception detection skills, they estimated a 77% level of accuracy, an unproven figure that indicates that faith in their abilities and their training is significantly skewed (Kassin, Leo, Meissner et al. 2007).

Content Analysis

One way to evaluate truthfulness and deceit in a subject is to focus on statement analysis and linguistic markers that may appear in oral and written statements or transcripts of audio recordings of interviews and interrogations. The analysis of statements from witnesses, victims, informants, persons of interest, or suspects involves evaluating first what these subjects choose to include or exclude from their storyline accounts; second, the manner in which they choose to express the information, including the sequence they select to recall the event; and, third, the use of what are termed as *moderating linguistic* or *verbal markers* (Sandoval, Matsumoto, Hwang et al. 2015).

Statement Analysis

Statement analysis is based on the theory that truthful statements or accounts of events based on actual memories differ from those based on fabricated accounts (Undeutsch 1989). From that perspective alone, deceivers face a number of challenges. They must decide what to reveal, what to omit, what to fabricate, and what they want to protect.

In general, truthful narrative accounts commonly possess four major elements. The first is an introductory statement, where the subject sets the stage for the main incident under investigation. Second is the main event, which also identifies victims, witnesses, and serves as the baseline primary memory. The third element is a concluding wrap-up to the narrative, which helps to further amplify activities or feelings of the subject after the main event took place. The final element is out-of-sequence information, which frequently happens when primary memories stimulate secondary memories at the scene of a crime or major event. The inclusion of secondary memories of an account validates the primary memory.

In contrast, deceptive narratives purposely omit information and are less detailed or sketchy than truthful ones. And deceivers typically deflect answering questions by injecting irrelevant or extraneous information into discussions that has nothing to do with the particular question asked. Why do liars limit the amount of their falsehood or omissions? Because no liar lies unnecessarily. Lying requires the liar to fabricate information, and if someone fabricates a storyline or deliberately omits information, it requires the person to recall the lie or omission accurately in subsequent questioning. Moreover, there is limited out-of-sequence information because most of the time, the lie is rehearsed in sequential, chronological order; recalling out-of-sequence events may further confuse the liar and muddle his or her storyline. Creating unnecessary filler information requires the liar to tell even more lies to recall later.

Another differentiating quality to look for between truthful and deceptive narratives or testimony is the inclusion or exclusion of thoughts and emotions at the time of the event and the recalling of these later. Most of us cannot recall a traumatic event in our lives without recalling feelings and emotions. They are part of the human experience. Liars have their hands full trying to recall the action side of their storyline, never mind the feelings and emotions that accompany their fabricated story. This emphasis on action over feelings and emotions is common to deceptive subjects.

Verbal Markers

Aside from the sequencing of the storyline and what a deceiver may decide to omit or fabricate in a narrative, the appearance of certain words, particularly certain adverbs, and the frequent use of nonprompted negation in narratives serve, in many cases, as representative indicators of deception according to an article by Sandoval, Matsumoto, Hwang et al. (2015). The article "Exploiting Verbal Markers of Deception across Ethnic Lines: An Investigative Tool for Cross-Cultural Interviewing" explains that:

- Words such as *maybe, kind of, sort of,* and *perhaps* are most associated with equivocation and are intentionally used by deceivers to distance themselves from the act of lying by tempering their responses.
- Words such as *no, did not, never, could not,* and *would not* in response to a simple open-ended question such as "Tell me what you did last Thursday?" imply deceit by avoiding a direct response to the question and by defensively focusing on what a person did not do rather than explaining what the person did do.

- Words such as *very*, *really*, *truthfully*, and *honestly* in narratives are used by writers and speakers to convince another person of something.
- Words such as *only*, *just*, *simply*, and *merely* are used to downplay or minimize the role of the speaker or writer.
- Words such as *then*, *after*, *next*, *while*, *so*, and *when* suggest an attempt to intentionally omit information that may be critical to the investigation.

A key finding of the article is that linguistic or verbal markers transcend ethnic or cultural differences among speakers of English as a second language, an important point to consider as our nation continues to grow in its cultural and ethnic diversity.

When examining narratives, interrogators or investigators are looking for inconsistency in the storyline. This process is facilitated when the investigator or interrogator possesses sufficient factual background knowledge of the case, possesses evidence, and has available statements from other persons familiar with the event under investigation. Additionally, such investigators or interrogators may rely on linguistic markers if they are sufficiently distinctive. When the investigator or interrogator possesses no factual information, when he or she has no alternative statements for comparison, and when the linguistic markers are not remarkable, nonverbal cues can become more important.

Avoid Focusing on the Wrong Nonverbal Cues

Researchers in behavioral science, the military, law enforcement, intelligence, and business communities have spent decades and multimillions, perhaps billions, of dollars searching for reliable and relevant nonverbal cues for detecting deception and lies in people. Despite their best efforts, they continue to come up short. More than 130 well-known empirically based studies conclude that there is no single nonverbal cue uniquely related to deception. In other words, there are no reliable universal cues such as Pinocchio's nose, which grows each time the subject lies (Vrij, Granhag & Porter 2010).

> All those books and videos promising to teach you how to spot liars through body language? None have empirical support. (DeSteno 2014a)

Yet law enforcement continues to retain an overreliance on nonverbal cues in its effort to detect lies and deception through observation of emotion-driven responses in subjects during an interrogation or custodial interview.

In this approach, liars were assumed to fear being caught and fear is associated with obvious physiological changes in the deceiver's body that do not appear in truth-tellers. Most police investigation manuals have several chapters devoted to nonverbal cues, often accompanied by photographs, which continue to postulate that liars are far more nervous than truth-tellers and will reveal their nervousness through telltale signs such as eye aversion, fidgeting, heightened anxiety, despair, increased perspiration, rapid heart rate, and defensive or submissive postural reflex responses or even anger (Inbau, Reid, Buckley et al. 2013).

The flaw in this emotion-driven theory is the continuing myth that deceivers or liars demonstrate far more nervous behaviors than innocent subjects or truth-tellers. As a further step in this approach, follow-on questions are strategically injected by interrogators to further heighten the emotional response and elicit verbal responses that affirm the interrogator's underlying assumptions of deceit and guilt in the subject.

The emotion-based approach has its limitations. First, experiencing emotion is not exclusive to liars. Truth-tellers also experience the same emotions, especially if they sense that their storyline or claims of innocence are not believed by the interrogator. Second, the follow-on investigative questions that are deliberately introduced are commonly framed in ways that further elevate the emotional responses in liars, but are theorized not to influence truth-tellers. Yet according to the National Research Council, no such differentiating question technique exists to date and it is doubtful that such questions can ever be developed (National Research Council 2003). Third, while there may exist behavioral indicators differentiating truth-tellers from liars, such cues are unreliable and too faint. Moreover, practiced deceivers may try to control their behaviors, emphasizing verbal and nonverbal cues that make them appear credible. Rather than trying to focus on universal nonverbal cues, another suggested approach is to identify nonverbal cues unique to the individual (DePaulo, Lindsay, Malone et al. 2003).

For Different People, Look for Different Cues

Recent research shows that people demonstrate deception cues unique to themselves and that the same person may show different deception cues under different occasions. So avoid using universal fixed models of body movements to detect deception in people. One more thing: tied to this approach is the understanding that verbal and nonverbal indicators may significantly change for each person, under different settings, and under different circumstances.

So how do we go about identifying the subject's baseline nonverbal cues and speech patterns to differentiate lies from truth? Current legacy training manuals suggest that the interrogator and investigator rely on small talk during the pre-interrogation or noncustodial interview and while in the process of trying to establish rapport. Yet responding to questions during a casual conversation is very different from responding to questions during an interrogation or custodial interview about a crime or terrorist plot. To overcome this challenge, one suggestion is to frame a series of questions purposely designed to generate baseline "truthful" responses under comparable stress conditions and in the same physical setting that the subject may experience during the interrogation (Vrij, Granhag & Porter 2010). Such baseline positive response behaviors may then help to discern truth from lies when the subject is deceitful.

Another point to keep in mind is to recognize that people may react differently to different investigators or interrogators, which implies that they may be truthful to one and lie to another. Additionally, people respond differently to different topics, depending on how personal the topic relates to them. Keep in mind, too, that a subject's nonverbal and verbal responses may change over time and, if interviewed on more than one occasion, may change over repeated interviews (Vrij, Granhag & Porter 2010).

The bottom line is that all nonverbal and verbal responses or behaviors are specific to the individual. Each person has his or her set of behaviors that occur when he or she is lying or telling the truth. And to identify baseline behaviors that differentiate between falsehoods and truth, focus first on identifying the subject's baseline truthful responses under the same sort of setting as the anticipated custodial interview or interrogation. To do this, though, you will need to spend enough time to get to know the subject before the start of the formal interrogation.

More Reliable Ways to Uncover Deceit

Based largely on work of Professor Aldert Vrij, of the University of Portsmouth in England, and his colleagues, the next two approaches have proven themselves in both research and field tests. The first is the *information-gathering interview*, and the second approach we will discuss is *imposing a cognitive load* (Vrij, Granhag & Porter 2010).

The Information-Gathering Interview Style

Most traditional or legacy police training manuals emphasize the "accusatory approach" to investigative interviewing or interrogations. In the accusatory approach, the interrogator or investigator confronts the subject with accusations, such as "You know that you did it. I know you did it. Now, let's get on with you telling me the truth." Typically, such an approach leads the criminal subject to respond defensively and in fairly short expressions, such as "I didn't do anything."

During a typical information-gathering interview, the interviewer asks broad open-ended questions that require detailed statements from the subject, such as "What did you do yesterday between 3:00 and 4:00 PM?" Like the cognitive interview technique, discussed in Chapter 5, the information-gathering interview approach commonly leads to the gathering of far more useful information and longer engaged responses from the subject than the former accusatory approach.

According to Vrij, Granhag & Porter (2010), the information-gathering response is also far more responsive to uncovering lies. First, it permits greater opportunities to check inconsistencies in the subject's storyline against the available evidence because of the detailed responses required of the subject. Second, it permits an opportunity to gather more nonverbal cues than the accusatory model because the typical interview is simply longer. Third, longer stories also afford opportunities to gather more verbal cues associated with deceit. Fourth, the absence of an accusatory, judgmental tone by the interviewer lessens duress in the subject and helps to serve as a safeguard against false confessions (Vrij, Granhag & Porter 2010). Yet, in its basic form, multiple studies have shown that aims of the information-gathering methodology are best accomplished when coupled with techniques that impose cognitive loads on the subject during questioning.

Imposing a Cognitive Load

A necessary complement to the information-gathering methodology is the need to impose a "cognitive load" in the subject. Here, the underlying assumption is that lying is more difficult than truth-telling. By increasing the cognitive load in suspected deceitful subjects, they will have fewer cognitive resources available to them to craft or sustain the lies. Two suggested ways for accomplishing this are: first, by asking the subjects to tell their stories in reverse order and, second, by insisting that the subjects maintain eye contact with the interviewer.

Requiring subjects to tell their stories in reverse order runs counter to the natural forward sequencing of events. Because liars already have depleted cognitive resources and energies by lying and deceit, they should find this unfamiliar mental exercise even more taxing than truth-tellers do. And insisting that subjects maintain continuous eye contact while telling their stories is distracting and makes a false narrative even more difficult to recall (Vrij, Granhag & Porter 2010). Another advantage is that maintaining eye contact with the subject facilitates the reading of facial expressions.

Evaluating Inconsistencies in Facial Expressions

All people express emotions on their faces in similar ways. Facial expressions are universal and independent of race, culture, ethnicity, nationality, gender, age, religion, or any other demographic variable. Moreover, unless deliberately planned to deceive, they are often immediate, automatic, and unconscious reactions. Advocates believe that learning to read such facial expressions means having a window into the soul of almost anyone. It is a powerful tool for investigators because facial expressions of emotion, among which there are seven, are the closest thing humans have to a universal language (see the following figure) (Matsumoto, Hwang, Skinner et al. 2011).

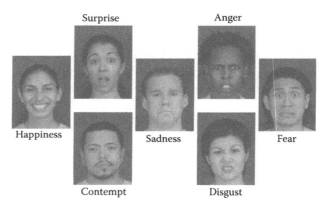

The seven basic emotions and their universal expressions. (From Matsumoto, D., H. S. Hwang, L. Skinner, and M. Frank, "Evaluating truthfulness and detection deception," *FBI Law Enforcement Bulletin*, June 2011, http://www.fbi.gov/stats-services /publications/law-enforcement-bulletin/june_2011/june-2011-leb.pdf.)

Those focused on facial expressions look for inconsistency between facial expressions and verbal expressions. For example, if while interviewing a subject, investigators or interrogators see an expression inconsistent with the words spoken or the emotions described, they should follow up until they can achieve reconciliation or get a more complete answer. This might include a subject showing disgust when talking about another person. What does that mean? It depends on the context. A subject giving a statement such as "He's a great guy" while his facial expression says otherwise may suggest that the subject is possibly lying. Regardless of the reason, something about the other person has produced an involuntary reaction in the subject. If interrogators can isolate and identify disconnects between the narrative and facial expressions, they can leverage them to clarify what really happened.

Uncovering Deception in Tandem Conspirators

One significant limitation in most deception research is that it examines deception as an exclusively individual-level phenomenon tied to a single deceiver. Yet encounters among intelligence collectors and law enforcement investigators frequently take place in field settings where an initial screening may likely include the opportunity to question two tandem witnesses or co-conspirators together. Such an opportunity presents a unique window for two suspects or witnesses to be interviewed in a group setting instead of separating them.

Typically, interviewing tandem conspirators has its risks, and isolating two or more companions is carried out ostensibly to remove them from the ability to collaborate on a storyline. Yet research studies by Driskell, Blickensderfer, and Salas (2012) and Driskell and Driskell (2013) suggest that there may be advantages to performing field interviews of two conspirators or witnesses simultaneously—particularly in an effort to uncover deception. The research studies suggest unique nonverbal and verbal cues to deception exist between accomplices that may not exist when interviewing them individually.

For example, do you recall seeing on television the video surveillance clips of the Boston bombers, the Tsarnaev brothers, strolling through a cheering downtown marathon crowd on April 15, 2013, carrying their pressure cooker bombs in backpacks shortly before they ignited their explosives? What if a law enforcement official had stopped to question them at that point? Would red flags have surfaced in their responses to questions that would have led the police to detain them for further questioning? Said another way, if you jointly questioned these two persons regarding their activities, with the bombs still concealed in their backpacks, would they have exhibited speech and behavior cues between themselves that might have indicated deception?

The preliminary research of Driskell, Blickensderfer, and Salas (2012) suggests that the looks and sounds of deceit existing between tandem conspirators at a group level that may not be apparent when these persons are interviewed or observed individually. For example, interactive behaviors—such as acknowledgments, back-channel responses, and corrections—may serve as cues to deception during their interactions when questioned together. Such cues are simply not observable on an individual level. The findings also suggest that two people typically describe an event differently when they actually experienced an event together versus when they did not and try to fabricate a story.

Truth-tellers are able to draw on their shared memory of the actual event that they experienced and would be able to describe this event in an interactive and collaborative manner. In other words, if you and I share some experience, say that we go on a fishing trip together, we encode memories of that event between ourselves. That is, you store in memory some parts of the event, and I store some parts. When we are questioned about the event, we recall it also in a joint manner—you recall some information, and I recall some information. Our style of interaction when recalling this jointly experienced event is collaborative—we elaborate on each other's sentences and fill in stories for one another. Collaboration and interaction are not as evident when two people recall a fabricated story that did not take place. Deceivers are more likely to describe the fabricated event from an individual perspective. In contrast to those that are truth-tellers, deceivers were also less likely to conduct back-and-forth exchanges, less likely to look at one another, and less likely to exhibit synchrony in communication (the degree to which one member of the twosome exhibits similar behaviors and uses similar linguistic styles as the other member).

Other Ways to Outsmart Liars

Time Well Spent

One proven principle involves the element of time spent with the detainee or suspect and the opening up of an ongoing dialogue. Quite simply, the more time the investigator or interrogator spends talking to a subject, the more information will be learned and the stronger the rapport between the two. Such chats may have nothing to do with the event or crime under investigation and could just easily focus on a casual chat over a beverage, meal, sporting event, or television show. As generally understood, once a suspect or detainee begins talking to an investigator or intelligence officer, the flow of words, in many instances, will eventually lead to the truth.

Being a Good Listener

Practice good listening skills. Be open minded to the person sitting before you, and seek to learn and understand from not only what the person is saying but also how it is being said. As a reminder, too, when asking questions, the investigator or interrogator should just listen and avoid any attempt to influence the recall of events. Again, empirical studies and research continue to emphasize the value of opening an investigative interview or interrogation with broad, open-ended questions followed by closed-ended clarifying or probing questions. The selective use of clarifying or closed-ended questions seeks to draw out further information about the event or act and should be reserved and held back until the subject concludes his or her response to the broad open-ended question.

Draw Me a Picture

Ask subjects to draw a picture of the event. Putting pencil to paper forces people to give spatial information—something that most liars are not prepared to do. Again, along with their lies, drawing pictures can overtax their mental resources. In general, drawings from liars are much less detailed than those of the truth-tellers—and are frequently at odds with their verbal testimony and the evidence (Vrij, Granhag, Mann et al. 2011). The use of drawings has other obvious benefits. First, it does not involve speech so that it can be used in interviews with interviewees who are not fluent in the language of the interviewer. Second, a drawing can be assessed immediately and does not require transcribing audiotapes (often necessary in speech analyses) or analyzing videotapes (often necessary in behavioral analyses). Third, a drawing can easily be checked for factual accuracy. Fourth, a drawing can be sketched in a relatively short period of time, which saves an interviewer's time.

Strategic Use of Evidence

Many legacy police methodologies fail to recognize the relevance of strategic use of evidence as an effective deception detection tool. For instance, many training manuals suggest officers confront suspects early on during an interrogation with the evidence in their possession to demonstrate the futility of remaining silent and not disclosing what they know. By doing so, however, they have handed a deceiver an unintended advantage.

One of the challenges liars face is uncertainty about the knowledge held by the investigator or interrogator. This makes it tough for a deceiver to know what they can say without the risk of offering statements in conflict with the evidence and known facts. If police officers disclose what they know too early during an interrogation, they reduce this uncertainty and make it easier for guilty suspects to change their stories and give alternative explanations for their ties to the evidence.

Recent research by Maria Hartwig and her colleagues reveals that early release in the interrogation process actually hampers lie detection. The results demonstrate that strategically timed release of evidence after the suspect has had ample opportunity to tell his or her side of the story dramatically improves opportunities for an interrogator or investigator to show inconsistency between the liar's storyline and the known facts or evidence and serves as valid cues to deception. And, initial research results are promising, with success rates as high as 67.6% for the interviewers' abilities to discern truth-tellers from liars by pinpointing duplicity and deception between the suspect's storyline and what the evidence reveals (Hartwig 2005).

Calling for a Code of Ethics

8

The continuing public debate over law enforcement, military, and intelligence interrogation programs demonstrates a number of shortcomings within the profession on a number of fronts. Let's face it; it is difficult to mention the word *interrogation* without conjuring up preconceived notions and disturbing mental images. Some issues are being addressed by the government through the legislative process and by sponsoring additional empirical-based research to identify improvements in current techniques and practices. Other initiatives may include establishing a basic core curriculum with certification, credentials, and oversight provided by the Special Task Force on Interrogations or the High-Value Interrogation Group. Then, too, is the need to formally professionalize the profession by requiring those who practice the tradecraft—whether on a full-time or a part-time basis—to comply with a common code of ethics.

The Need for a Code of Ethics

Most dictionaries and related professional manuals define *profession* as an occupation or trade requiring "specialized knowledge" typically after intensive study, leading to a shared understanding among practitioners. Such references further define a *professional* as someone who complies with "technical and ethical standards of a profession."

The term *ethics* is generally used to describe someone's conscience or moral fiber. One who possesses ethics is said to know right from wrong and can be trusted to make the right decision in unfamiliar and unsupervised circumstances in which there are no easy answers. Anecdotal evidence seems to suggest that those who lack ethics face a host of personal and professional challenges.

For a profession, a code of ethics operates much the same way as a person's conscience. Professionals in many occupations are guided by them—a set of principles by which they practice their professions on behalf of those who entrust to them an important duty or responsibility. For instance, the legal and medical professions are two examples that come to mind. Doctors swear a commitment to the Hippocratic Oath, which requires physicians to uphold certain standards of their profession. Likewise, lawyers are expected to comply with the rules of professional conduct issued by the American Bar Association. Encouraging the establishment of a common ethical code shared among interrogators—regardless of whether he or she is in law enforcement, the military, or the intelligence community—would serve as an important step toward remedying some of the major shortcomings identified by critics over the past several decades.

A common code of ethics will forge a unifying bond among all interrogators; instill a sense of pride in the profession; serve as a moral compass in those unique moments when there is not sufficient guidance or precedent; and, for those who fall short and violate the public trust, permit the profession to revoke credentials. In other words, a code of ethics will serve as the profession's ethos. It will keep the profession in check by reminding those within it of their duty to the nation, to the U.S. Constitution, and to our laws and related international agreements.

Leading the Change

The Department of Justice, the Department of Defense, and the Office of the Director of National Intelligence ought to share responsibility as principal stakeholders to drive the formulation of a code of ethics for our nation's interrogation program on behalf of the American people. Each possesses a vested interest in it. In taking on this overdue initiative, the three institutions would help close an apparent void within the profession. And, in this case, a code of ethics would not just help to distinguish between right and wrong but, in a wider sense of the word, would be used to describe the underlying guideposts and distinctive culture of the profession. The following figure is offered to assist in its formulation.

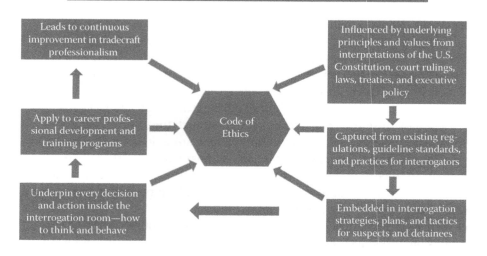

Importantly, too, a code of ethics is needed to help guide the profession for the road yet ahead and for a public safety and national security environment at home and abroad that remains uncertain and demanding; and anticipates continuing challenges for the profession in the future. Whatever the final version might look like, a suggested framework for a code of ethics would help:

- Define the basic principles that help guide practitioners in uncertain times and circumstances—now and into the future.
- Embrace an operational climate of high expectations and standards among practitioners and require humane treatment of suspects and detainees.
- Provide the shared profession a shared professional identity which encompasses a sacred trust among practitioners.
- Put practitioners on notice that those who violate the code of ethics would bring dishonor to themselves, to their cohorts, and to their profession, and likely result in the loss of their credentials and possibly expose them to civil and criminal liability.
- Recognize that the code of ethics would likely need periodic updates in faces of new legislation, judicial rulings, and executive policy decisions by our nation's leaders.
- Advance the profession by encouraging lifelong learning and continuous professional improvement among practitioners.

Final Thoughts

Before wrapping up our discussions on ethics, permit me to drive home an important point which, coincidentally, serves as a fitting end for this primer. That is, no matter where an interrogator serves—law enforcement, the military, or intelligence—and no matter the degree of expertise—entry-level trainee or a fully professionalized master interrogator, all share a responsibility to advance the profession and the tradecraft. And, this shared pledge to the profession and tradecraft is best exemplified by six simple words: **Do No Harm—Respect Human Rights**. A credo all interrogators should adopt and help promote throughout their careers.

Key References
and Suggested Readings

American Psychological Association (APA). 2014. *Resolution on Interrogations of Criminal Suspects.* http://www.apa.org/about/policy/interrogations.aspx.

Anyaso, H. H. 2012, December 6. *Deception Can Be Perfected.* Northwestern University News Center. http://www.northwestern.edu/newscenter/stories/2012/12/decep tion-can-be-perfected.html#sthash.q5O6UkzC.dpuf.

Army Field Manual 34–52. 1992. *Intelligence Interrogation.* Publicly available online. http://www.loc.gov/rr/frd/Military_Law/pdf/intel_interrrogation_sept-1992.pdf.

Army Field Manual 2–22.3. 2006. *Human Intelligence Collector Operations.* http:// armypubs.army.mil/doctrine/Active_FM.html.

Bond, C. F., Jr., and B. M. DePaulo. 2006. Accuracy of Deception Judgments, *Review of Personality and Social Psychology*, 10, 214–234.

Boumediene versus Bush, 553 U.S. 723. (2008).

Bram versus United States, 168 U.S. 532 (1897).

Brown versus Mississippi, 297 U.S. 278 (1936).

Bureau of Justice Assistance (BJA). 2011. *Plea and Charge Bargaining.* U.S. Department of Justice. Prepared by L. Devers, PhD, under government contract. https:// www.bja.gov/Publications/PleaBargainingResearchSummary.pdf.

Central Intelligence Agency (CIA). 2004. *Guidelines on Medical and Psychological Support to Rendition, Interrogation, and Detention.* Office of Medical Services. Formerly Top Secret, Declassified in 2005. Available online in multiple venues.

Chambers versus Florida, 309 U.S. 227 (1940).

Central Intelligence Agency (CIA). 2014. *CIA Comments on the Senate Select Committee on Intelligence Report on the Rendition, Detention, and Interrogation Program.* Director of Central Intelligence. Formerly Secret. Signed June 27, 2013, and released unclassified to the public on December 8, 2014. https:// www.cia.gov/mobile/news/2014/CIAs_June2013_Response_to_the_SSCI _Study_on_the_Former_Detention_and_Interrogation_Program.pdf.

Cialdini, R. B. 1984. *Influence—The Psychology of Persuasion.* William Morrow: New York, NY.

Delia, J. 2008. *Constructivism: A First Look at Communication Theory.* E. Griffin. McGraw-Hill: New York, NY.

Department of Justice (DOJ). 2009. *Special Task Force on Interrogations and Transfer Policies Issues Its Recommendations to the President.* Press release August 24, 2009. http://usdoj.gov/opa/pr/2009/August/09-ag-835.html.

Department of Justice (DOJ). 2014. BJS Bulletin: Prisoners in 2013. E. Ann Carson, Ph.D., *Bureau of Justice Statistics.* Updated September 30, 2014.

DePaulo, B. M., J. L. Lindsay, B. E. Malone, L. Muhlenbruck, K. Charlton, and H. Cooper. 2003. Cues to Deception. *Psychological Bulletin*, 129, 74–118.

DeSteno, D. 2014a, March. Who Can You Trust? *Harvard Business Review*. HBR Reprint R1403K.

DeSteno, D. 2014b, June. The Simplest Way to Build Trust. *Harvard Business Review*. https://hbr.org/2014/06/the-simplest-way-to-build-trust.

Dillon, J. T. 1990. *The Practice of Questioning*. Routledge Publishing: London.

Driskell, J. E., and T. Driskell. 2013, October. Gathering Information in Field Settings: A Social Dynamics Approach. *The Military Psychologist*. American Psychology Association: Washington, DC.

Driskell, T., E. L. Blickensderfer, and E. Salas. 2012. Is Three a Crowd? Examining Rapport in Investigative Interviews, Group Dynamics: Theory, Research, and Practice. *American Psychological Association*, 17, 1, 1–13.

Drizin, S. A., and R. A. Leo. 2004. The Problem of Confessions in the Post-DNA World. *North Carolina Law Review*, 82.

Educing Information: Interrogation: Science and Art (Phase I). 2006, December. Intelligence Science Board. National Defense Intelligence College Press: Washington, DC. http://www.fas.org/irp/dni/educing.pdf.

Evans, J. R., K. A. Houston, and C. A. Meissner. 2012, April. A Positive, Collaborative, and Theoretically-Based Approach to Improving Deception Detection. *Journal of Applied Research in Memory and Cognition*. University of Texas. http://www.katehouston.com/Evans%20Houston%20and%20Meissner%20JARMAC.pdf.

Evans, J. R., C. A. Meissner, S. E. Brandon, M. B. Russano, and S. M. Kleinman. 2010, Spring–Summer. Criminal versus HUMINT Interrogations: The Importance of Psychological Science to Improving Interrogative Practice. *The Journal of Psychiatry & Law*, 38, 215–249. http://plx.sagepub.com/content/38/1-2/215.full.pdf+html.

Farber, I. E., H. F. Harlow, and L. J. West. 1957. Brainwashing, Conditioning, and DDD (Debility, Dependency and Dread). *Sociometry*, 20, 4, 271–285.

Fisher, R. P., and R. E. Geiselman. 1992. *Memory Enhancing Techniques for Investigative Interviewing: The Cognitive Interview*. Charles C. Thomas: Springfield, IL.

Fisher, R. P., and R. E. Geiselman. 2010. The Cognitive Interview Method of Conducting Police Interviews: Eliciting Extensive Information and Promoting Therapeutic Jurisprudence. *International Journal of Law and Psychiatry*, 321–328.

Fisher, R., and D. Shapiro. 2005. *Beyond Reason: Using Emotions as You Negotiate*. Penguin Books: USA.

Garcia, J. M. 2009, September. *Renditions: Constraints Imposed by Laws on Torture*. Congressional Research Service. RL32890. http://www.loc.gov/crsinfo.

Gladwell, M. 2005. *Blink: The Power of Thinking without Thinking*. Little Brown and Company: New York, NY.

Gudjonsson, G. H., and M. Hilton. 1998. The Effects of Instructional Manipulation on Interrogative Suggestibility. *Social Behaviour*, 4, 1989, 189–193.

Hamdan versus Rumsfeld, 548 U.S. 557 (2006).

Hartwig, M. 2005. *Interrogating to detect deception and truth: Effects of strategic use of evidence*. Department of Psychology, Göteborg University, Sweden.

Heuback, J. 2009, December. *Suspect Interrogation: Communication Strategies and Key Personality Constructs.* Kansas State University. http://www.k-state.edu /actr/2010/12/20/suspect-interrogation-communication-strategies-and-key -personality-constructs-jessica-heuback/default.htm.

Hinkle, L. E., Jr., and H. G. Wolff. 1957, September. The Methods of Interrogation and Indoctrination Used by Communist State Police. *Bulletin of the New York Academy of Medicine.* http://www.ncbi.nlm.nih.gov/pmc/articles/PMC1806200/.

Hu, X., H. Chen, and G. Fu. 2012, December. A Repeated Lie Becomes a Truth? The Effect of Intentional Control and Training on Deception. *Frontiers in Psychology.* http://www.ncbi.nlm.nih.gov/pmc/articles/PMC3495335/.

Inbau, F. E., J. E. Reid, J. P. Buckley, and B. C. Jayne. 2013. *Criminal Interrogations and Confessions.* Fifth Edition. Jones and Bartlett Learning: Burlington, MA.

Intelligence Interviewing: Teaching Papers and Case Studies (Phase II). 2009, April. Intelligence Science Board. National Defense Intelligence College Press: Washington, DC. http://fas.org/irp/dni/isb/interview.pdf.

Interrogation: World War II, Vietnam, and Iraq. 2008, September. Center for Strategic Intelligence. National Defense Intelligence College Press: Washington, DC. Electronic copies are available at http://www.ndic.edu. Approved for unrestricted distribution by the Office of Security Review in the Department of Defense.

Interview with Andrew Tahmooressi. 7 November 2014. Broadcast on Fox News Network. http://insider.foxnews.com/2014/11/06/marine-sgt-andrew-tahmooressi -goes-record-exclusive-interview-after-his-release-prison.

Interview with Michael Koubi: Israeli Interrogator. 17 November 2004. *New Scientist.* http://www.newscientist.com/article/mg18424745.700-interview-michael -koubi-israeli-interrogator.html.

Interview with Stephen Kleinman. 2 November 2007. An Interview: Senior Intelligence Office, U.S. Air Force. http://www2.gwu.edu/~nsarchiv/torturingdemocracy /interviews/steven_kleinman.html.

Jolie, A. 2014, December. *Unbroken.* Universal Films. Based on the book *Unbroken* (2010) by Laura Hillenbrand.

Kassin, S. M. 2012. Why Confessions Trump Innocence. *American Psychologist,* 67, 6.

Kassin, S. M., and C. T. Fong. 1999. "I'm Innocent!": Effects of Training on Judgements of Truth and Deception in the Interrogation Room, *Law and Human Behavior,* 27, 499–516.

Kassin, S. M., R. A. Leo, C. A. Meissner, K. D. Richman, L. H. Colwell, A. M. Leach, and D. La Fon. 2007. Police Interviewing and Interrogation: A Self-Report Survey of Police Practices and Beliefs. *American Psychology—Law Society* (Division 41 of the American Psychological Association).

Knowles, E. S., and J. A. Linn. 2004. *Resistance and Persuasion.* Lawrence Erlbaum: Mahwah, NJ.

Konnikova, M. 2015, February. You Have No Idea What Happened. *The New Yorker.* http://www.newyorker.com/science/maria-konnikova/idea-happened-memory -recollection.

KUBARK Counterintelligence Manual. 1963. Central Intelligence Agency. Declassified from Secret and released January 1997. Available online in multiple venues.

Leave No Marks: Enhanced Interrogation Techniques and the Risk of Criminality. 2007. Physicians for Human Rights and Human Rights First, Washington, DC.

Leo, R. A. 1992. *From Coercion to Deception: The Changing Nature of Police Interrogation in America.* University of California. Also published in *Crime, Law and Social Change,* 18, 1–2, 35–59, September 1992.

Leo, R. A. 1996. Inside the Interrogation Room. *The Journal of Criminal Law and Criminology,* 86, 2, 266–303.

Leo, R. A. 2009. False Confessions: Causes, Consequences and Implications. *The Journal of the American Academy of Psychiatry and the Law.* Available at http://works.bepress.com/richardleo/1.

Leo, R. A., and Oshfe, R. J. 1998. Consequences of False Confessions: Deprivations of Liberty and Miscarriages of Justice in the Age of Psychological Interrogation. *The Journal of Criminal Law & Criminology,* 88, 2, Northwestern University School of Law.

Loftus, E. F. 2011. Intelligence Gathering Post-9/11. *American Psychologist,* 66, 532–541.

Matsumoto, D., H. S. Hwang, L. Skinner, and M. Frank. 2011, June. Evaluating Truthfulness and Detection Deception. *FBI Law Enforcement Bulletin.* http://www.fbi.gov/stats-services/publications/law-enforcement-bulletin/june_2011/june-2011-leb.pdf

McCain, J. 2005, November. Excerpt from Senate speech in support of the Detainee Treatment Act of 2005.

McCain, J. 2014, December. Excerpt from Senate floor statement made in reference to the release of the Senate Select Intelligence Committee Report on CIA interrogation methods.

McLeod, S. A. 2010. *Cognitive Interview.* http://www.simplypsychology.org/cognitive-interview.html.

Meissner, C. A., J. R. Evans, S. E. Brandon, M. B. Russano, and S. M. Kleinman. 2010. Criminal versus HUMINT Interrogations: The Importance of Psychological Science to Improving Interrogative Practice, *Journal of Psychiatry & Law,* 38, 215–249.

Meissner, C. A., A. D. Redlich, S. Bhatt, and S. Brandon. 2012, September 1. *Interview and Interrogation Methods and Their Effects on Investigative Outcomes.* Campbell Crime and Justice Group.

Miller versus Fenton, 797 F.2d 598 (1986).

Miranda versus Arizona, 384 U.S. 436 (1966).

Mitchell, B. 1983, September. Confessions and Police Interrogations of Suspects. *Criminal Law Review,* 596–604.

Moston, S. J. 1996. From Denial to Admission in Police Questioning of Suspects. In *Psychology, Law and Criminal Justice,* G. Davies et al. (eds.). Walter de Gruyter: Berlin, 1996, 92.

Mueller, D. H. 2014, July. The Importance of Witness Recall in Avoiding Wrongful Convictions. *American Psychology—Law Society* (Division 41 of the American Psychological Association).

National Research Council. 2003. *The Polygraph and Lie Detection.* Washington, DC: National Academic Press.

Neubauer, D. W. 1974. Confessions in Prairie City: Some Causes and Effects. *Journal of Criminal Law and Criminology*, 65, 1974, 103–112.

Office of Legislative Research (OLR). 2008, January 8. *Crime Rate and Conviction Rates Broken Down by Race*. 20008-R-0008. Prepared for the Connecticut General Assembly. http://www.cga.ct.gov/olr/.

Phillips, C., and D. Brown. 1998. *Entry into the Criminal Justice System: A Survey of Police Arrests and Their Outcomes*. Home Office Research, 185. HMSO: London.

Plon, H. (ed.). 1861. *Correspondence Napoleon*. 1861. Vol. V, 3606, 128.

Possley, M. 2012. *Darrel Parker: The National Registry of Exonerations*. A Project of the University of Michigan Law School. https://www.law.umich.edu/special/exoneration/Pages/casedetail.aspx?caseid=4015.

Rafaeli, A. 1991, December. Emotional Contrast Strategies as Means of Social Influence: Lessons from Criminal Interrogators and Bill Collectors. *The Academy of Management Journal*, 34, 4, 749–775.

Redlich, A., A. Summers, and S. Hoover. 2009. *Self-Reported False Confessions and False Guilty Pleas among Offenders with Mental Illness*. American Psychology Law Association.

Rochin versus California, 342 U.S.165 (1952).

Ross, H. J. 2014. *Everyday Bias: Identifying and Navigating Unconscious Judgments in Our Daily Lives*. The Rowan & Littlefield Publishing Group Inc.: Lanham, MD.

Royal, R. F., and S. R. Schutt. 1976, August. *The Gentle Art of Interviewing and Interrogation: A Professional Manual and Guide*. Prentice-Hall: Upper Saddle River, NJ.

Sandoval, T., D. Matsumoto, H. C. Hwang, and L. Skinner. 2015, July. Exploiting Verbal Markers across Ethnic Lines: An Investigative Tool for Cross-Cultural Interviewing. *FBI Law Enforcement Bulletin*. https://leb.fbi.gov/2015/july.

Skolnick, J. H., and R. A. Leo. 1992, Winter/Spring. The Ethics of Deceptive Interrogation. *Criminal Justice Ethics*, 2, 1, 3–12.

Stephenson, M. T., and K. Witte. 1997. *Fear, Threat, and Perceptions of Efficacy from Frightening Skin Cancer Messages*. Texas A&M University.

The Economist. 1998, June 11. Fred Inbau: Obituary. http://www.economist.com/node/135414.

The Innocence Project. 2015. A nonprofit legal clinic affiliated with the Benjamin N. Cardozo School of Law at Yeshiva University. http://www.innocenceproject.org/about/.

The National Registry of Exonerations. 2015. A project of the University of Michigan Law School. http://www.law.umich.edu/special/exoneration/Pages/casedetail.aspx?caseid=4015.

Tickle-Degnen, L., and R. Rosenthal. 1990. The Nature of Rapport and its Nonverbal Correlates. *Psychological Inquiry*, 1, 285–293.

Tourison, S. D., Jr. 1991. *Talking with Victor Charlie: An Interrogator's Story*. Ballantine Books: New York, NY.

Undeutsch, U. 1989. The Development of Statement Reality Analysis. In *Credibility Assessments*, J. C. Yulie (ed.). New York, NY.

U.S. Congress. 2008, November. *Inquiry into the Treatment of Detainees in U.S. Custody.* Senate Armed Service Committee. See: http://www.armed-services .senate.gov/imo/media/doc/Detainee-Report-Final_April-22-2009.pdf.

U.S. Congress. 2014, April. *Committee Study on the Central Intelligence Agency's Detention and Interrogation Program.* Senate Select Committee on Intelligence. See: http://www.intelligence.senate.gov/study2014/sscistudy1.pdf.

Vent versus State, 67 P.3d 661/Alaska Ct. App. (2003).

Vrij, A., A. Granhag, and S. Porter. 2010. Pitfalls and Opportunities in Nonverbal and Verbal Lie Detection. *Association of Psychological Science.*

Vrij, A., P. A. Granhag, S. Mann, and S. Leal. 2011, February. Outsmarting the Liars: Toward a Cognitive Lie Detection Approach. *Current Directions in Psychological Science,* 20, 1, 28–32.

Walsh, D., and R. Bull. 2012. Examining Rapport in Investigative Interviews with Suspects: Does Its Building and Maintenance Work? *Journal of Police Criminal Psychology,* 27, 73–84.

White House. 2009, January. *Executive Order 13491: Ensuring Lawful Interrogations.* https://www.whitehouse.gov/the_press_office/Ensuring_Lawful_Interrogations.

White House. 2009, April. *Statement of President Obama on Release of OLC Memos.* Office of the Press Secretary. http://www.whitehouse.gov/the_press_office /Statement-of-President-Barack-Obama-on-Release-of-OLC-Memos/.

Wright, J. 2013, September. Applying Miranda's Public Safety Exception to Dzhokar Tsarnaev: Restricting Criminal Procedure Rights by Expanding Judicial Exceptions. *Columbia Law Review Sidebar,* 113, 136–155. http://columbialawreview .org/boston-bombers-miranda-rights_wright/.

Index

Printed in Australia
AUHW011043010223
374056AU00035B/179

9 781498 751148